cosmic mba series

entrepreneurs
toolkit

Rory Burke

rory@burkepublishing

Entrepreneurs Toolkit
Rory Burke
ISBN 0-9582391-4-2

Published: 2006

Distributors: UK: Gazelle Books, email: sales@gazellebooks.co.uk
               USA: Partners Book Distributing, email: partnersbk@aol.com
               South Africa: Blue Weaver Marketing, email: orders@blueweaver.co.za
               Australia: Thames and Hudson, email: orders@thaust.com.au

DTP: Sandra Burke
Cover Design: Simon Larkin (Jag Graphics)
Sketches: Tang, Woric, Ingrid, Buddy Mendis, Rory Birk
Printer: Everbest, China

Production notes: Page size (168 x 244 mm), Body Text (Adobe Garamond Pro 12 point), Chapter Headings (Arial, 30 point), Subheadings (Arial, bold, 12 point), Software InDesign CS, Photoshop CS, Illustrator CS, CorelDRAW12, Dell and Mac notebook computers.

ISBN: 0-9582391-4-2

Dedication:.....*to my mentor Kirk, who is always ready to drop in when I have a problem!*

Content

Lifestyle Entrepreneur

Rory Burke was educated at Wicklow and Oswestry. He has an MSc in Project Management (Henley) and degrees in Naval Architecture (Southampton) and Computer Aided Engineering (Coventry). Rory has worked on marine and offshore projects in Britain, South Africa, the Middle East and New Zealand.

After dreaming about bluewater cruising for twenty years, Rory finally decided to take the plunge and go for an entrepreneurial lifestyle. He discovered that the bluewater adventure made history and geography come alive as he followed in the footsteps of the great explorers.

The bluewater lifestyle has given Rory a sense of adventure where he feels he is living life to the full and allows him more time to focus on his research and writing. Where better to experience street entrepreneurs at source, where the first world meets the third world, and be able to negotiate with necessity entrepreneurs thriving in a black market economy.

BBC interview

To continue their bluewater lifestyle, Rory and Sandra have set up a publishing company, which they run from their yacht – a truly mobile office in the South Pacific.

To keep in touch with the 'real world', Rory is a visiting lecturer to universities in the UK, Australia, South Africa, Canada, America, Hong Kong and Singapore.

Cosmic MBA Series - content

Entrepreneurs Toolkit	Small Business Entrepreneur
ISBN 0-9582391-4-2	ISBN 0-9582391-6-9
Entrepreneur BOK	Small Business BOK
Entrepreneur Spiral	Staircase to Wealth
Do We Really Need Entrepreneurs?	What Type of Work
Who Wants To Be An Entrepreneur	Buying a Business
Entrepreneur Traits	Franchise Business
Creative Ideas	Family Business
Innovation Process	Working from Home
Catching the Wave	Outsourcing
Marketing	Registering a Small Business
Networking	Financial Statements
Negotiation	Business Plan
Sources of Finance	Estimating Techniques
Managing Growth	Accounts and Cash Flow
Risk Management	Sales and Marketing
	Distribution
	Customer Service

Cosmic MBA Series - content

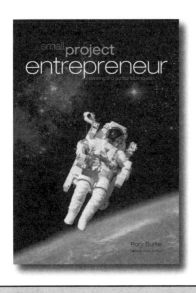

Small Project Entrepreneur	Team Building Entrepreneur
ISBN 0-9582391-1-8	ISBN 0-9582391-8-5
Small Project BOK	Team Building BOK
Product Life-Cycle	Teamwork
Plan and Control Cycle	Team Member Selection
WBS	Team Development Phases
CPM	Leadership Styles
Gantt Chart	Power to the People
Procurement	Motivating the Team
Resources	Delegation
Cash-Flow	Problem-Solving
Communication	Decision-Making
Quality Control Plan	Creativity and Innovation
Risk Management	Resistance to Change
Control (problem-solving)	Conflict Resolution
Crashing	Communication
Earned Value	Indoor Team Building
Computers	Outdoor Team Building
OBS / Matrix	Appendix - NASA Moon Landing

Foreword

In 25 years of business experience I have encountered many different characters – clever strategists, sharp lawyers, tough operators – however, the one type that I have found both impressive and intriguing are the **entrepreneurs.**

One thing is certain: we all recognise the entrepreneur. From the card swapper in the school playground, Ghanaian street entrepreneurs selling cell-phone time, to such universally recognised business icons as Bill Gates or Richard Branson – entrepreneurs stick out from the herd. We are captivated by their spirit, their abilities and, more often than not, by their successes.

Entrepreneurs are central to the human condition – featuring even as the subject of one of President George W. Bush's most widely circulated linguistic gaffes. Bush is said to have proclaimed, *"The problem with the French is that they don't have a word for entrepreneur."* – whether this says more about Bush, the French or entrepreneurs will keep pundits arguing for many years. Notwithstanding that, it shows that entrepreneurs and their role in society command attention.

I have been watching a few episodes of the current TV series based around a well known businessman and a group of hopefuls competing for an apprenticeship. This captures some of the thrill surrounding the entrepreneur but the demands of TV mean it is edited down to stress emotions and does not allow a careful analysis of the workings of entrepreneurship.

"....The problem with the French is that they don't have a word for entrepreneur...."

What makes an entrepreneur? For some people it is a gift of nature; like great sportsmen they are endowed with the skills, determination and insight that make it all work. That said, observation and study of entrepreneurs demonstrate there are basic techniques and skills that can be learnt to allow anyone to raise their own entrepreneurial skills in a range of situations.

I was honoured to be asked by my cousin, Rory Burke, to write this forward. Rory is a true man for all seasons. His career has followed an entrepreneurial path. He has looked for opportunities, evaluated risks and exploited circumstances. He has had a wealth of experience, encompassing commercial project management, building houses, circumnavigating the globe and setting up his own publishing business.

In these books on entrepreneurship Rory has set out his own insight and experience to enable you, the readers, to share these with the aim of improving your entrepreneurial skills – to use in whatever field of activity that you choose.

Successful application of these skills may win you a significant return on the effort invested in learning from these books – maybe even, in some cases equal to the fabulous returns of the business icons who symbolise entrepreneurship for us all.

Alex Minford

Alex read Modern History at Exeter College Oxford where he first encountered **entrepreneurship** *running a cocktail business. As a Chartered Accountant - he worked with Touche Ross and now works for Elsevier. Alex commutes from his lifestyle farm house in South Wales to London and Amsterdam.*

Authors Note

With your head buzzing with innovative and creative ideas - welcome to the entrepreneur's world of spotting opportunities, networking and setting up new ventures. These desirable traits are increasingly seen as the difference between proactive companies growing and creating wealth, and reactive companies resisting change and 'hanging-in there' hoping to avoid the scrap heap.

Entrepreneurs are increasingly being acknowledged by Governments as the driving force behind innovative change and job creation. In our deregulated and competitive world the small business entrepreneur can now compete on a level playing field with large corporations - it used to be 'the big eat the small' but now it is 'the fast assassinate the slow'.

Business schools have responded to the demand for entrepreneurs by including entrepreneurship and business enterprise modules in many of their courses. The rationale being that when students graduate they can use these entrepreneurial skills to help establish their careers.

With the wave of entrepreneurship growing I realised there was an opportunity to write a series of books which focused on the entrepreneur's tools and techniques, their application, and the entrepreneur's behaviour and traits.

This is the first book on the launch pad - *Entrepreneurs Toolkit* - which focuses on the tools and techniques the entrepreneur can use to identify opportunities, test the market, raise finance, and grow the business.

One of the unique features of *Entrepreneur Toolkit* is that it uses plenty of diagrams to visually present the entrepreneurial business environment. This makes it much easier and quicker for the reader to assimilate the concepts. Two of these graphically presented concepts are:

- Entrepreneurship body of knowledge which is presented as a structured breakdown
- Entrepreneurial spiral which is a novel way of showing the logical relationship between the management topics.

Writing the cosmic mba series has enabled me to subdivide the key management topics into a number of stand alone books linked by the common thread of entrepreneurship. In practise, no one management topic can really stand on its own for long - at some point the entrepreneur will need to use the other management skills.

Why call it the Cosmic MBA Series? Exploring the cosmos has always been the final frontier, and an excellent example of how man can use their entrepreneurial skills to meet the ultimate challenge. This series is one small step to extend the library of entrepreneurial tools and techniques. And also a great opportunity to design some dynamic looking book covers (thanks Simon).

An **Instructor's Manual** is available for lecturers with additional exercises and case studies, see <www.knowledgezone.net>. The Knowledge Zone web site has been set up to hold the educational resources for all our publications.

Acknowledgements: I have been researching this book for the past few years and wish to thank all the entrepreneurs and lecturers I have networked with around the world. I particularly wish to thank Steve Barron (Lancaster University), David Farwell (University of South Australia), Peter Mellalieu and Howard Frederick (Unitec), and Mark Massyn (University of Cape Town).

For proof reading I wish to thank Kirk Phillips (my mentor) and Jan Hamon (Jan insisted I refer to entrepreneurs as 'he'), and for the inspirational foreword Alex and Louise Minford.

Rory Burke

Lifestyle Entrepreneur, currently in the South Pacific 37°S 175°E

1
Entrepreneurship Body of Knowledge

LEARNING OUTCOMES - enables the reader to:

Define entrepreneurship.

Present the entrepreneurship body of knowledge as a breakdown structure.

Show how entrepreneurship is interrelated with project management, small business management, team building and risk management.

Compare and contrast the entrepreneur's management style with a production manager's management style.

With your head buzzing with innovative and creative ideas - welcome to the entrepreneurs' world of spotting opportunities, networking and setting up new ventures. These desirable traits are increasingly seen as the difference between proactive companies growing and creating wealth, and reactive companies resisting change and 'hanging-in there' hoping to avoid the scrap heap. Entrepreneurs are increasingly seen as the driving force behind innovative change in our society.

Entrepreneurs are usually associated with small businesses operating in a niche market. This book will explain how we can all be entrepreneurs at one time or another, whether we are managing a small business, managing a large corporation, or are streetwise necessity entrepreneurs. Entrepreneurs are also found managing welfare ventures, social ventures, sports ventures, and even adventure projects. Entrepreneurship, more than anything, is an attitude – a proactive management approach to seizing opportunities and getting things done.

Entrepreneur millionaires always seem to capture our imagination – making us envious and motivated at the same time. Their success often seems obvious to us after the event. For example, selling mobile phone ring tones is a multi-million business, *"Why didn't I think of that?"* Well you probably did, but due to a combination of laziness, procrastination and fear of taking a punt, you did nothing about it!

1. What is Entrepreneurship?

Entrepreneurship is a developing management topic which has yet to formally produce a **body of knowledge** to ringfence the boundary of knowledge areas (see page 16). There are, however, many eloquent definitions for *'entrepreneur'* and *'entrepreneurship'* which can be used to gain an appreciation of its meaning and scope.

'Entrepreneur' is a French word which dates back to the 1700s. Since then it has evolved to mean someone who **undertakes a venture**, particularly a new venture, and this is central to the use and understanding of the word *entrepreneur* in the English language. Apparently the French prefer to use *'createur d'entreprise'*.

Jean-Baptiste Say, a French economist of the 1800s stated that, "…. *an entrepreneur shifts economic resources out of an area of lower productivity into an area of higher productivity and greater yield.*" This sounds very similar to Pareto's 80/20 analysis, where 80% of an entrepreneur's income comes from 20% of their clients or their work. The motivation is to focus on the 20% that gives the greatest return, and move away from the 80% that gives the lowest return.

The Oxford Dictionary describes the entrepreneur as; *'…. one who organises, manages and assumes the risks of a business enterprise'*. This definition identifies the entrepreneur as the key person managing the entrepreneurial process. This could involve co-ordinating, planning and controlling the input of suppliers, contractors and team members. This definition also acknowledges the entrepreneur's willingness to accept the risk and uncertainties for the success of the new venture.

Bolton and Thompson, from the University of Huddersfield, describe an entrepreneur as; *'…. a person who habitually creates and innovates to build something of recognised value around perceived opportunities'*. The word *'habitually'* implies innovation is something the entrepreneur is continually doing – it is not a one off event. This definition also states that if the product is not valued by the market, then the endeavour will be a failure.

Chaston, from the Plymouth Business School, describes entrepreneurship as; '*.... the behaviours exhibited by an individual and / or organisation which adopts a philosophy of challenging established market conventions during the process of developing new solutions*'. This definition points out that entrepreneurship is not restricted to an individual - entrepreneurship can also be an approach to managing a large company. The definition also highlights that the innovative challenge is a disruptive approach to changing the existing status quo.

Hall, from Durham University Business School, describes an entrepreneur as; '*.... someone who starts and builds something of long-term value, often from practically nothing. Usually an unsung hero*'. This definition implies that entrepreneurs are not all after a quick buck, they genuinely want to see their creation being useful and stand the test of time. This definition also suggests that entrepreneurs often operate quietly behind the scenes, and very few of them desire to be high profile business people such as Richard Branson (Virgin), Bill Gates (Microsoft) and Anita Roddick (Body Shop).

Porter, the great American economist, advises that; '*.... innovation and entrepreneurs are at the heart of economic advantage*'. Michael Porter is well known for saying that the success of a company is directly related to achieving competitive advantage. This comment confirms that entrepreneurs and innovation are the driving force behind companies striving to achieve competitive advantage.

Burns, from Luton Business School, advises that; '*.... as the business grows and the scale of activities increases, the entrepreneur has to learn to delegate*'. It is a surprising fact that rapid growth can be the achilles' heel of many entrepreneurs – their reluctance to seed power, delegate and use integrated management systems can lead to a success-disaster where the success of increased sales leads to a production and distribution nightmare.

This book will take a broad view of entrepreneurship and define it as a management technique or approach, which actively encourages creative ideas, and searches for marketable opportunities to set up new ventures, solve problems, or more generally, look for ways of improving our way of life. The entrepreneur is the key person making the decisions and accepting the risks, but also looks for an attractive return on his investment.

It is common to talk of someone being an entrepreneur as if implying a management style and behaviour rather than an organisational position. '*Senior Entrepreneur*' positions are never advertised in the press, although, there are many job descriptions that call for creativity, innovation, risk taking and dynamic leadership. These are generally considered to be classic entrepreneurial traits.

Entrepreneurs are normally associated with the small business environment, however, it is important to point out that entrepreneurs abound in all walks of life. Consider these categories below to determine if there is an entrepreneur within you trying to break out:

Corporate Entrepreneurs: Large corporations are increasingly recognising that they need the entrepreneurial spirit to keep their products and company at the leading edge of technology and prevent their organisation becoming overly bogged down with head office bureaucracy. Jack Welch is a classic corporate entrepreneur who turned General Electric (GE) around from a $13 billion company to a $550 billion company in 20 years.

Street Entrepreneurs: Street entrepreneurs abound in all societies. They are particularly active in the third world and informal markets, where they keep the wheels of industry and commerce turning. Who would have thought that a dentist could market his trade by displaying piles of extracted molars on a table in a Moroccan souk, as he awaits another brave customer? These are necessity entrepreneurs using their streetwise savvy to make ends meet.

Social Entrepreneurs: Many successful entrepreneurs move from accumulating wealth in their formative years to distributing wealth in their later years. Andrew Carnegie is reported to have said, "*The man who dies rich, dies disgraced*". Carnegie himself disposed of 90% of his wealth before he died. Other well known social entrepreneurs include Dr Barnardo who founded homes for orphaned children, and William Booth who founded the Salvation Army which looks after the homeless. I always give generously to the Sallies - just in case.

Adventure Entrepreneurs: The great explorers such as David Livingstone and Captain Cook were adventure entrepreneurs who took enormous risks to extend the boundaries of human discovery. Other great adventure entrepreneurs include Ernest Shackleton whose exploits and leadership in the Antarctic caught our imagination; Edmund Hillary who was the first mountaineer to climbed Mt Everest; and Neil Armstrong who put man's first footprint on the moon.

2. Body of Knowledge (bok)

The Body of Knowledge of a profession is an inclusive term used to describe the sum of knowledge within the profession. As with other professions such as project management and accounting, the body of knowledge rests with the practitioners who use it. The body of knowledge identifies and describes the generally accepted practices for which there is widespread consensus of their value and usefulness. It also establishes a common lexicon of terms and expressions used within the profession.

Although the entrepreneurial spirit has been a key feature in our evolution and industrial development, as a management profession it is still relatively new and has yet to formally define a body of knowledge. However, the definitions of entrepreneurship in the previous section point to a number of knowledge areas and management topics, which are presented as a structured breakdown in figure 1.1. These collectively form the body of knowledge and the backbone of this book.

Entrepreneur: In figure 1.1 the entrepreneur's traits are identified as a knowledge area because the entrepreneur creates the innovative changes and spots the opportunities that drive new ventures. The entrepreneur is the key person, the linchpin, the person who makes-it-happen. The entrepreneur's character and behaviour are discussed in the *Entrepreneur Traits* chapter.

Opportunities: Creative ideas, innovation and problem-solving combine to form the opportunities knowledge area. Entrepreneurs often use lateral thinking methods (thinking outside the square) to generate novel solutions, and they are always looking for marketable opportunities. The opportunities knowledge area is discussed in the following chapters; *Creative Ideas, Innovation Process,* and *Catching The Wave.*

Marketing: Great innovative ideas that do not sell, and ingenious solutions that are rejected, are failures in terms of entrepreneurship. In contrast, poor ideas that sell well and weak solutions that are accepted, are deemed an entrepreneurial success. The *Marketing* chapter will show that it is essential for the entrepreneur to ensure there is a market for their product or service. The potential market should obviously be determined at the outset. In fact the entrepreneur is unlikely to raise funds and venture capital unless the business plan clearly presents a convincing marketing strategy. The entrepreneur must be able to take the product or service to market and sell it.

Networking: Networking skills are possibly the most important entrepreneurial trait determining entrepreneurial success. The entrepreneur's ability to develop a

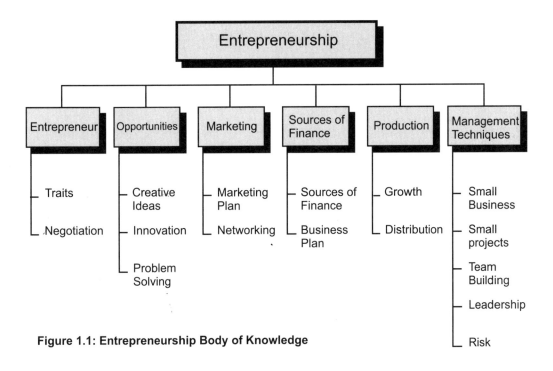

Figure 1.1: Entrepreneurship Body of Knowledge

network of helpful contacts far outweighs any portfolio of academic degrees and certificates of employment. The '*old-school-tie*' - who you know, has always been acknowledged as being more important than what you know. The *Networking* chapter will discuss how the entrepreneur identifies and develops relationships with their key stakeholders.

Negotiation: Negotiation is the art of influencing people to make them see things your way!!! The *Negotiation* chapter discusses the win-win strategy as a collaborative approach where each party is trying to achieve the best deal for both parties - a mutually agreeable solution. This chapter also discusses negotiation tactics and dispute resolution.

Sources of Finance: Acquiring sufficient funding is a key component of any entrepreneurial venture. Without financial support and investment, innovative ideas and marketing opportunities cannot be developed, and may simply fall by the wayside as lost opportunities for another entrepreneur to pursue. Most entrepreneurial ventures need some form of financial support to oil the wheels of development - to produce the prototype, to test the market, and to get the production facilities up and running. The *Sources of Finance* chapter will discuss a range of debt and equity options.

Business Plan: As creative ideas and opportunities evolve into marketable products, at some point the entrepreneur needs to formalise his approach with a coherent business plan. The structure of the business plan is set out in the *Sources of Finance* chapter. These topics will be developed further in my *Small Business Entrepreneur* book.

Production: In figure 1.1 the production knowledge area covers the manufacture and distribution of a product. Many entrepreneurial projects start with developing a prototype to test the product's performance and confirm that it can be built or produced. This obviously relates to the technical content and scope of the new venture. It must be stressed that, if the entrepreneur cannot produce a quality product that meets the clients needs, is competitive, reliable, and professionally supported by a willing customer service, then the whole entrepreneurial endeavour will be self-limited.

Research suggests entrepreneurs do not search for '*state of the art*' equipment or the '*best material available*' to develop their products or services, but rather they use equipment and materials that are sufficient to complete the project. Far from being perfectionists, entrepreneurs are **pragmatists** who put together the minimum resources required to perform the job quickly and effectively to meet their clients' needs, and make a respectable profit.

Entrepreneurs are experts at **cutting corners** and getting away with it. They are **streetwise** bargain hunters always looking for a good deal on resources and materials to give them competitive advantage. This ensures they not only give their client a good deal, but they also make an attractive profit at the same time.

Managing Growth: Managing growth is the achilles' heel for the typical entrepreneur – while the business is small he can manage everything in his head on a day-to-day basis. But with rapid growth, the entrepreneur's ad hoc leadership style needs to change to a more formalised management approach, to enable effective planning and control. And here-in lies the problem - entrepreneurs by their very nature are motivated by opportunities, freedom, risk and profit - whereas production managers are motivated by resources, delegation and security (see figure 1.4).

The *Managing Growth* chapter discusses why growth companies are so important to the economy and are the darlings of the stock market, particularly for an IPO (Initial Public Offering). Their rapid growth not only sucks in large amounts of resources and funding, but also creates plenty of employment and ultimately expands the economy.

3. Entrepreneur Management Techniques

There are a number of management techniques the entrepreneur needs to include in his portfolio of business and management skills, to ensure he is able to manage a new venture effectively. Four of these core management topics highlighted in the body of knowledge are presented below as intersecting circles within an entrepreneurial environment.

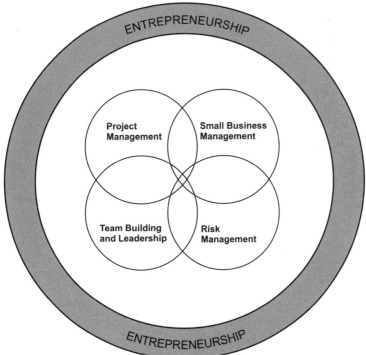

Figure 1.2: Entrepreneur Portfolio of Management Techniques

Figure 1.2 shows how project management, small business management, team building and leadership, and risk management are core management topics under the entrepreneurship umbrella.

- Project management skills are required to plan and control the new venture.
- Small business management skills are required to manage a company on a day-to-day basis.
- Team building and leadership skills are required to inspire, build and lead a team.
- Risk management skills are required to assess, monitor and respond to risk and uncertainty.

All these topics come together to form the entrepreneur's portfolio of business and management skills.

4. Project Management

Setting up a new venture has all the characteristics of a small project which requires effective project management skills to plan and control the entrepreneurial process. Managing a small project is not necessarily a scaled down version of a large project. Although small projects may appear to be simpler and more straight forward - they often have their own unique problems:

- lack of definition - no drawings, no specifications and no contract
- instructions given verbally - nothing in writing to confirm agreements
- minimum standards not established - making it difficult to enforce quality control requirements to accept or reject the work
- no arbitration mechanisms - making it difficult to quickly and amicably sort out any disputes
- no exit strategies - making it difficult to terminate the contract
- short duration - this does not give the entrepreneur time to establish a management system and learn by his mistakes.

The entrepreneur has a multitude of challenges to face when implementing a new venture, so it is important to ensure innovative ideas and opportunities are not handicapped at the outset by ineffective project management. Many creative ideas have floundered because of unrealistic expectations, communication breakdown, poor co-ordination and uncontrolled cash-flow.

Project managers use a number of special project management techniques to plan and control the progress on their projects. These should form an important part of the entrepreneur's portfolio of management skills:

- **Work Breakdown Structures** [WBS] to quantify the scope of work and subdivide the scope into manageable work packages.
- **Critical Path Method** [CPM] to graphically present the logical relationship between activities; to calculate the activities' start dates, finish dates and float; to identify the critical path of activities which determines the duration of the project.
- **Gantt Charts** [barcharts] to graphically present the scheduled information and assign the activities to the person, department or company responsible for each activity.
- **Procurement Schedule** to graphically link the materials and equipment requirements to the schedule, and to highlight any long lead items which could delay the schedule.
- **Resource Histograms** to graphically link the resource requirement to the schedule, and to highlight any overloads and underloads which may require resource smoothing.

- **Earned Value** [EV] to graphically present the integration of the planned manhours, the earned manhours and the actual manhours against the schedule.
- **Quality Control Plan** [QCP] to link the specifications and level of inspection to the sequence of work.
- **Organisation Breakdown Structure** [OBS] to graphically overlay the temporary project team structure on the functional organisation structure - usually presented as a matrix structure.
- **Configuration Management** to manage scope changes, which includes; logging the proposed changes, approving the changes, and implementing the changes.
- **Document Control** to plan and control the flow of documents, which includes; establishing a list of documents to be controlled, collating the documents, storing the documents, issuing the documents with a transmittal note, and withdrawing old documents.

All these special project management techniques are integrated into the planning and control cycle as shown in figure 1.3. These techniques are explained in my book *Project Management Planning and Control Techniques*.

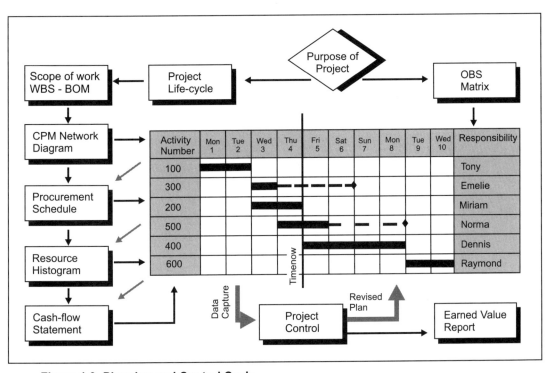

Figure 1.3: Planning and Control Cycle

5. Small Business Management

Entrepreneurs and small business managers are often thought of as being one and the same. But in practice entrepreneurship is the management of change, particularly when starting a new venture or introducing a new product or service. Whereas, small business management is the management of the company on a day-to-day basis - particularly with respect to repetitive jobs. Some of the key small business management functions include:

- marketing the company and the products
- accounts, budgets, book-keeping and cash flow
- paying wages, invoices and debtors
- complying with rules, regulations and taxes
- buying or renting premises
- buying, leasing or hiring plant and equipment
- procurement of material and services
- warehousing and stock control (JIT)
- distribution
- labour relations, recruitment and hiring
- supervision and leadership
- manufacturing the product (technical), and scheduling the workflow
- quality control
- customer service.

Entrepreneurship and small business management obviously go hand-in-hand, and may be seen as two sides of the same coin. Small businesses swing in and out of periods of entrepreneurial change as the business introduces new products, then consolidates its gains, before repeating the cycle at the next opportunity. For example, entrepreneurial change would include the starting of the business, the development of new products, the introduction of new management systems and the penetration of new markets. But, after each entrepreneurial change, the small business would need to consolidate the change and continue at the new level until there is a need or opportunity to change again.

In practice the true entrepreneur would get bored running a small business that did not continually challenge the status quo. These topics will be covered in detail in my book on *Small Business Entrepreneur*.

6. Teamwork and Leadership

The entrepreneur is the driving force behind a new venture - leading, co-ordinating, managing and organising the input of suppliers, contractors and team members. This requires:

- leadership skills to communicate the vision
- inspiration to motivate the team to work towards a common goal
- influence and power to make the work happen.

New ventures, by their very nature, require that extra push to overcome a minefield of obstacles and challenges associated with changing the status quo. Entrepreneurs need to build management teams for a number of reasons:

- to increase the number of people available to match the workload as outlined in the resource plan
- the nature of the work may require a range of complementary skills which any one person is unlikely to have
- to solve problems - interactive team work and brainstorming encourages cross-fertilisation and synergy, where the team generates more and better ideas than people acting on their own
- to make decisions - gain collective commitment and resources from the team members
- to enhance motivation - team cohesiveness will motivate team members to give 110% and not let the side down
- risk taking - management teams generally make riskier decisions than an individual would because there is a feeling of mutual support and sharing of implications.

The entrepreneur, as team leader, is responsible for building an effective team that has the technical skills required to do the work, together with a balance of appropriate human personalities and behaviours so that the team members can work effectively together. Team building incorporates a range of functions that the entrepreneur is responsible for:

- team design - to establish a resource profile of complementary skills
- team selection - psychometric testing to achieve a balance of human personalities and behaviours
- team building - to integrate the team to work effectively together
- team coaching and mentoring - guiding and encouraging each team member's performance
- succession planning and handover as players leave and new members join the team.

7. Risk Management

Developing new ideas, seizing opportunities and starting new ventures will always involve an element of risk and uncertainty, and things will go wrong from time to time. Although entrepreneurs are usually stereotyped as foolhardy risk takers - to understand how entrepreneurs manage their risks goes right to the heart of entrepreneurship. Risk management techniques are covered in detail in the *Risk Management* chapter.

8. Compare Management Styles

The successful entrepreneur needs to be able to vary his management style to reflect the needs of the new venture and the culture of the team, as the venture passes through the phases of the product life cycle (see chapter on *Managing Growth*). It is interesting to compare the different management styles and traits of an entrepreneur, and a production manager. During the setting up, development and growth phases of a company the entrepreneur may need all of these business and management skills and traits at one time or another.

ENTREPRENEUR	PRODUCTION MANAGER
Leads	Manages
Inspires	Administrates
Innovates	Maintains
Business Focused	Systems Focused
Sees Opportunities	Sees Problems
Has Informal Networks	Has Formal Communications
Self-Focused	Delegates
Takes Risks	Risk Adverse (Security)
Revolutionary	Evolutionary
Unpredictable Environment	Predictable Environment
Rents or Borrows Premises	Owns Premises

Figure 1.4: Comparing an Entrepreneur and a Production Manager's Management Styles

Exercises:

1. The body of knowledge ringfences the accepted practices of entrepreneurship. Discuss how these knowledge areas apply to you.

2. Entrepreneurs are said to be pragmatists. Discuss how you have cut corners to make a product and get it to market before the competition.

3. Project management is a core topic within the entrepreneurship umbrella. Discuss how you would plan and control a new venture.

Instructor's Manual: An Instructor's Manual is available with additional exercises and case studies, see *<www.knowledgezone.net>*.

2
Entrepreneurial
Spiral

LEARNING OUTCOMES - enables the reader to:

Draw the entrepreneurial spiral to show the entrepreneurial process.

Show how the entrepreneurial process can start from any of the four main management areas.

Show how the entrepreneurial spiral can be used to plan and control the entrepreneurial process.

Identify who is the entrepreneur.

The definitions of entrepreneurship developed in the previous chapter refer to a number of key management topics which, although they are usually presented on their own, are in fact inter-related. This chapter will take these definitions a step further and present entrepreneurship as a logical sequence of inter-related management topics where a change in one management topic may change the parameters in one or more of the other management topics. For example, if there is a delay in obtaining funding for a new venture, this could delay the release and marketing of the new product and could increase your risk by giving the competitors the chance to get their product to market first.

To present the logical sequence of inter-related management topics as a straight forward flow chart would be over simplifying the situation, because it would imply that each management topic is performed one after the other, and when you reach the bottom of the list you have finished.

In practice the human mind is much more complex. We have an amazing capacity to think about many things at the same time - consider how we solve crossword puzzles or play chess. A more realistic model which accommodates our thinking styles is an iterative spiral (see figure 2.1) where the management topics follow a logical loop. By repeating the loop many times each management topic can be developed progressively as the venture converges on an optimum solution.

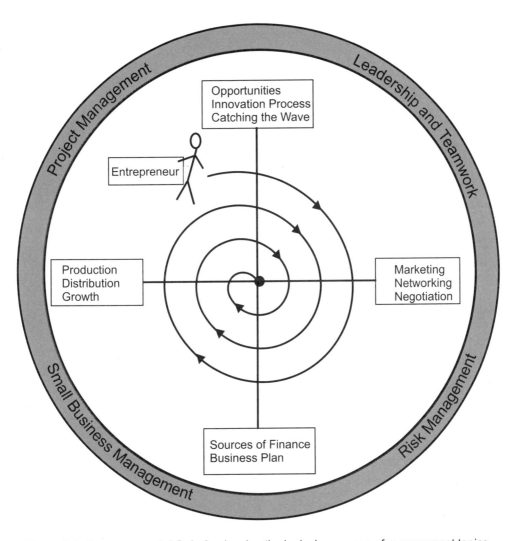

Figure 2.1: Entrepreneurial Spiral - showing the logical sequence of management topics surrounded by the entrepreneurial environment

The entrepreneurial spiral shows the four key management topics at the four cardinal points; Opportunities, Marketing, Sources of Finance, and Production. The direction of the arrows shows the logical sequence of the entrepreneurial process. The entrepreneurial environment is shown as a ring of management techniques which surrounds the spiral.

1. Entrepreneurial Spiral - Opportunities

The logical sequence of management topics shown in figure 2.2 outlines the classic entrepreneurial venture which starts with an opportunity or creative idea. This could be an inventor, working in his garage or shed, who creates a novel product similar to Trevor Baylis' windup radio (see *Creative Ideas* chapter for more information), or Steve Jobs' Apple computers. In this scenario the entrepreneurial process starts with the opportunity or invention of a new product, followed by the entrepreneur conducting market research to confirm there is a market for the product. The entrepreneur then arranges finance to fund the venture, and finally plans the manufacturing of the product.

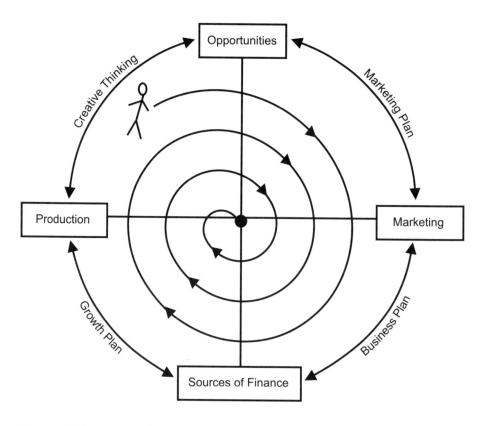

Figure 2.2: Entrepreneurial Spiral - starting with the Opportunity

2. Entrepreneurial Spiral - Marketing

The entrepreneurial venture could also start with the marketing function. Through a network of contacts, and market research, the entrepreneur could identify a gap in the market for a new product, and quickly seize the opportunity before the competitors. In this scenario the entrepreneurial spiral starts with feedback from the marketing function, followed by the entrepreneur arranging finance to fund the new venture. The entrepreneur then plans the manufacturing facilities to make the product and, finally, develops the product design to incorporate the latest opportunities and creative ideas.

Richard Branson's Virgin companies generally do not manufacture the products they are associated with - they are the marketing front. They negotiate naming rights to help the products gain a high profile, for example, Virgin Atlantic (transatlantic airline), Virgin Cola (similar to Coca Cola) and Virgin Mobile (telecommunications).

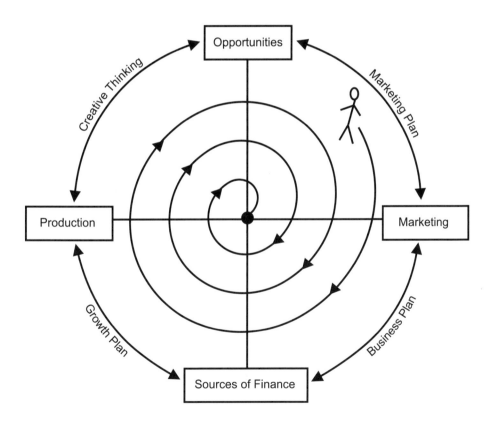

Figure 2.3: Entrepreneur Spiral - starting with Marketing

3. Entrepreneurial Spiral - Sources of Finance

The entrepreneurial spiral could also start with the sources of finance. Through a network of contacts the entrepreneur could be approached by a venture capital firm or a business angel, who has pockets bursting with cash, looking for an entrepreneurial venture in which to invest. In this scenario the entrepreneurial spiral starts with the availability of funds, followed by the entrepreneur planning the manufacture of the product. The entrepreneur then designs the product to incorporate the latest opportunities and creative ideas, and finally conducts market research to confirm there is a market for the product.

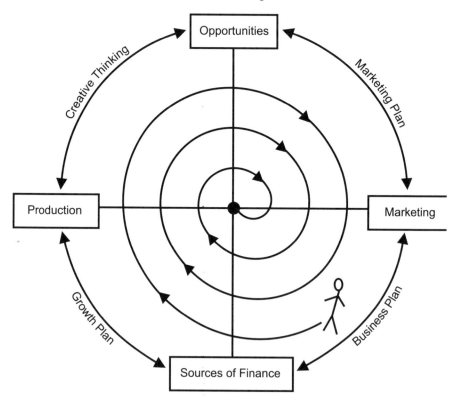

Figure 2.4: Entrepreneurial Spiral - starting with the Sources of Finance

4. Entrepreneurial Spiral - Production

The entrepreneurial spiral could also start with the production function. Through a network of contacts, the entrepreneur could be approached by the owner of a company who has underutilized manufacturing facilities and resources, such as; machines lying idle, staff without assignments, or material left over from previous jobs. In this situation the need for work starts the entrepreneurial spiral, followed by the design of the product to incorporate the latest opportunities and creative ideas. The entrepreneur then conducts market research to confirm there is a market for the product, and finally arranges finance to fund the new venture. The manufacturer might even be encouraged to '*buy work*' by offering the company's resources at a competitive rate.

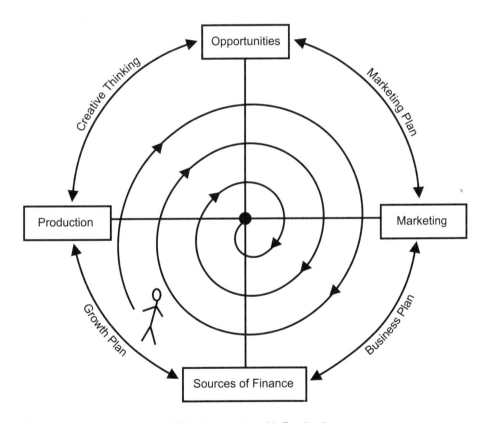

Figure 2.5: Entrepreneurial Spiral - starting with Production

5. Iterative Spiral

The logical sequence of work outlined in the previous sections might not always be the best sequence for the new venture. A feature of the entrepreneurial spiral is the iterative process whereby, with each revolution of the spiral, every logical sequence of the four managerial functions can be achieved. For example, consider the sequence set out in figure 2.6:

1. The entrepreneur's new venture starts with an opportunity or a creative idea for a new product or service.
2. The entrepreneur then bypasses the marketing function moving on to arranging the finance to fund the new venture.
3. The entrepreneur then bypasses the production and opportunities functions moving on to conducting the market research to confirm there is a market for the product.
4. The entrepreneur then bypasses the sources of finance function moving on to planning the manufacture of the product.

By leap-frogging past certain management functions, every possible sequence of work can be mapped out. Although this may seem like a convenient fix, it does at least enable the entrepreneur to graphically present an action plan which can be agreed, communicated, monitored and controlled. In effect the spiral becomes a planning and control document.

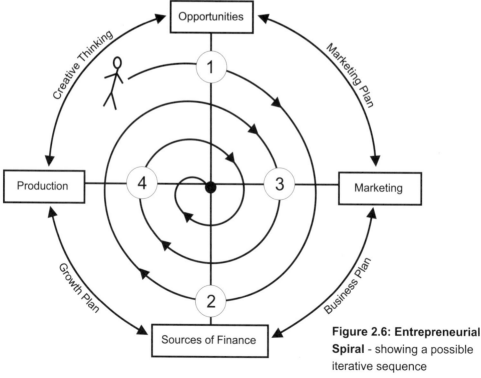

Figure 2.6: Entrepreneurial Spiral - showing a possible iterative sequence

6. Who is the Entrepreneur?

It seems logical to assume that the person who starts the ball rolling is the entrepreneur driving the new venture. From the previous examples this could be a manager from any of the four cardinal points (management topics). But what happens if the person starting the new venture does not have the management skills and the entrepreneurial 'X' factor to make-it-happen?

It is a common mistake to link technical ability with management ability. For example, if someone is a creative architect, this does not mean he will be an efficient project manager constructing the building he has designed. The creative skills an architect uses to design a building are completely different to the managerial skills an entrepreneur needs to plan and control the project. The success of the entrepreneurial project could therefore be self-limiting if the person starting the venture does not have the ability to manage the project and, further, insists on hanging on to the reins of power.

Another possibility is that the entrepreneur could be a third party (not from any of the four cardinal points) who co-ordinates and manages the input of the key players using a project team, or **matrix** organisation structure. In this arrangement, the entrepreneur becomes the **project manager**; the linchpin who provides the leadership catalyst and pulls all the project players together. This is one of the reasons project management is a core subject within the entrepreneurship body of knowledge.

Co-ordinating new ventures may require a certain amount of leadership and project management ability to make-it-happen, particularly if the entrepreneur needs to involve other people (suppliers and contractors), and definitely if the new venture needs to raise capital.

Exercises:

1. Give examples of the entrepreneurial process by starting a new venture at each of the four cardinal points.

2. Use the iterative spiral format (figure 2.6) to give an example of a new venture which uses a different sequence to question 1.

3. Give an example of a new venture where the entrepreneur (project manager) is a third party to the entrepreneurial process and co-ordinates the input of suppliers, contractors and team members.

Instructor's Manual: An Instructor's Manual is available with additional exercises and case studies, see <*www.knowledgezone.net*>.

3
Do We Really Need Entrepreneurs?

LEARNING OUTCOMES - enables the reader to:
Discuss why large companies need entrepreneurs.
Explain why mature companies need entrepreneurs.
Discuss how privatisation and deregulation have freed up the market for entrepreneurs to compete on a level playing field.
Outline why red tape and compliance costs are disproportionately onerous for small businesses.

What would the world be like without entrepreneurs? Would we still be in the stone age living like troglodytes. Have we benefited from the entrepreneurs' ability to spot innovative opportunities and their drive to make-it-happen?

The motivation to write this book was the belief that entrepreneurs do make a difference - a big difference for the better. The supporting argument is that entrepreneurs have the ability to spot innovative opportunities to improve the economy and our society. They achieve this through their network of contacts, their drive, and their determination to make things happen. In today's competitive economy, if companies wish to stay in business they need to be continually changing to keep up with:

- new technology
- changing market needs
- changing management systems.

Just look around you and note what has changed in the past few years. For instance, music collections of cassettes have been replaced by CDs and MP3s (LPs and 45s records are long gone), and these in turn are under threat by Apple's iPod. Film collections are also changing - VHS video collections are presently being replaced with DVDs. And in a few years time, CDs and DVDs will almost certainly be replaced by some form of memory stick. The Internet, for example, has established a completely new communication and business platform within a decade!

Mobile phones are currently at the forefront of consumer technology and fashion. Who would have thought that an entrepreneur could become a millionaire by supplying mobile phone ring tones? Yet some enterprising entrepreneur spotted this opportunity and made himself a millionaire. This is a classic example of an entrepreneur spotting an opportunity within a market dominated by large multi-nationals like Vodafone and Orange.

The message is clear - if businesses are not developing new products they will be increasingly clinging on to obsolete technology. This is when the business needs that entrepreneurial flair to keep up to date with the latest technology and market trends.

1. Why Large Companies Need Entrepreneurs

The Fortune 500 list of American companies clearly shows what happens to big companies that do not innovate – they disappear!!! One third of the Fortune 500 industrial companies have left the list in the past 15 years. However, this does not necessarily mean they have actually gone out of business and closed down. More likely, due to their poor performance and a weak share price, they were taken over by an entrepreneurial company who thought it could turn them around.

In contrast, there are also companies in the Fortune 500 that have survived for 75 years or more. What is the key to their survival? The answer is - '*experiment in the margin*'. They are continually exploring new business products and opportunities that create potentially new sources of growth. They are not resting on their laurels or milking a cash cow.

Entrepreneurship is generally associated with small dynamic companies, but large companies can also be entrepreneurial. Take IBM for example; it set up a new business unit to develop the personal computer (circa 1980) which was so successful that it established a new market standard - the IBM PC. It also enabled Microsoft (the operating system supplier) to become the largest computer software company in America, and Bill Gates to become the richest entrepreneur in America.

One could argue the PC was not really an IBM project, as it was designed by an offshoot company set up by IBM to develop the PC. This is true, but you have got to give the IBM senior management credit for clearly spotting the opportunity for an open source desktop computer, and realising that their management structure was too bureaucratic to respond quickly enough to get the new computer to market before the competition.

A number of large airline companies have also taken a similar competitive strategy, by setting up small offshoot carriers with lower overheads to compete in the expanding budget carrier market.

2. Mature Companies

As companies develop and grow they pass through a number of recognizable phases of development; from start up to survival, growth to maturity, and eventually they go into decline (which may lead to either takeover, or liquidation and closure) see *Managing Growth* chapter, figure 13.1.

Unfortunately, company growth often leads to a creeping paralysis where systems and bureaucratic procedures become more important than the very creative ideas and innovation that originally underpinned the company's successful products. This results in the management of mature companies becoming bogged down in their own self-importance and red tape.

Instead of generating creative ideas, large bureaucratic companies can actually become idea killers, where rules and regulations take precedence over creativity and innovation. With innovation increasingly being eliminated from the corporate gene pool the HRM may find many of their bright graduates leaving in frustration.

Large companies invariably lose some of their best players who feel **frustrated** that the company is not responding to their creative ideas and the opportunities they have spotted. The final straw for these employees is when they see another company developing THEIR creative ideas - this famously happened at Xerox's R&D centre in Silicon Valley.

In this bureaucratic condition, the managers may be incapable of reacting swiftly to market trends, commercial opportunities and customer feedback. This is when the CEO needs to make an SOS call for an entrepreneur to introduce some

CEO ....."Help - my company has broken down - I urgently need an entrepreneur to fix it"

shock therapy to revitalize the company's strategy and increase performance. The entrepreneur's challenge is to reduce the bureaucracy that stifles creativity, and set the managers free to capture the innovation that abounds in their organisation.

This situation happened in the 80s when Jaguar Cars sent an SOS call to John Eagan, a corporate entrepreneur. Eagan used his entrepreneurial approach to identify where the resources and systems were not being used effectively. He motivated the staff and boosted their confidence by investing in new car designs and the latest manufacturing equipment, which in turn led to better products, a sense of achievement and, most importantly, the recognition that the company was producing world class cars again. Eagan also improved the quality and reliability of the cars, the lack of which had been a major complaint from their disillusioned customers. The result was increased sales, increased profits and a brand that regained its association with performance and excellence.

3. Industrial Revolution (take two)

The large state run industries of the 60s with their long assembly lines which mopped up unemployment, have been progressively privatised and automated. There has also been a refocus on competitive advantage with large companies outsourcing much of their non core work to small entrepreneurial businesses. All these entrepreneurial changes are offering the consumer an abundance of every conceivable product on the planet and, further, the products are being produced more efficiently, cheaper, and with automation by fewer people.

Since the mid 1970s there has been a shift from large companies competing through mass production and economy of scale towards smaller companies relying on knowledge, innovation and flexibility. We are currently witnessing a silent revolution where the **entrepreneurial economy is overtaking the managed economy.**

4. Privatisation and Deregulation

Margaret Thatcher's battle with the unions in the early 1980s, fast-tracked a revolutionary period of privatisation and deregulation of nationalised industries and monopoly corporations in Britain. This freed up the market for entrepreneurs to introduce new technology, new products and more efficient working practices.

The national airlines of the world are an excellent example of how privatisation and deregulation are encouraging efficiency, downsizing and reduced airfares. After years of limited landing rights and restrictions in the skies, the national airlines had grown big and bureaucratic with all the symptoms and inefficiencies associated with mature companies - some shock therapy was needed.

Several entrepreneurs spotted the opportunity and market need for small, no-frills, budget airlines. They cut back on non-essential services which lowered their overheads and, together with last minute airfare reductions, achieved high seat occupancy. They appealed to the budget traveller, and this is where the market is growing.

This entrepreneurial change happened around the world. In Australia, Virgin Blue (set up from scratch by Richard Branson) gained market share from Qantas (the national airline). In the UK, both Ryanair and easyJet gained market share from BA (the world's *'favourite airline'*). And in America, Southwest, and JetBlue gained market share from United Airlines and American Airlines (even though AA offers its economy passengers 33 inches of leg room).

The budget airlines achieved their cost advantage not just by being small and cutting back on in-flight services, but by being more entrepreneurial and efficient. Two-thirds of the budget airlines cost advantage comes from having superior, more economical business processes, such as selling seats over the Internet and flying their aircraft more hours each day. The large national airlines prefer hub-to-hub services, whereas the small airlines prefer point-to-point. The figures confirm point-to-point fly more hours than hub-to-hub services. And further, the no-frills airlines can turn around their planes in 25 minutes while the large national carriers take three times longer.

The entrepreneurial approach is to focus on core activities where the company can maximise its competitive advantage, and outsource all non core activities to other companies who specialise in those areas, such as cleaning, catering, security and baggage handling. Information technology, in its various forms, has given the budget airlines a way to cut operational costs while improving customer service.

Deregulation: The removal of competition limitations has spawned shoals of small innovative companies, not just in the airline industry but across the board. For every Freeserve, Egg or First Direct spun out of an existing banking business, there are ten or more new ventures set up by entrepreneurs who are unconstrained by the corporate culture of, *'this is the way we do things around here'*. For example, the online book store <www.Amazon.com> was not set up by a large book chain store like Borders or Barnes & Noble in America, nor was online Dell Computers, with its online procurement and built to order manufacturing process, set up by a large computer company like IBM.

".... I'll make sure you won't land at my airports"

Deregulation of restrictive practices has led to an explosive growth in small businesses. We are entering the entrepreneurial age again - not seen since the Victorian pioneering days of coal, steam and rail.

5. Red Tape

For a country to achieve economic growth it must establish a business environment that encourages entrepreneurship and small business enterprise development. A good place to do business is usually associated with:

- ease of setting up a company
- ease of raising finance
- ease of enforcing a contract
- ease of hiring and firing workers
- lack of red tape
- low business compliance costs.

Business compliance costs include time spent within the enterprise complying with tax requirements, employment-related requirements, environment-related requirements, plus the cost of external advice and any special labour costs such as, paid maternity leave and flexible working hours. These costs are disproportionately more onerous for the smaller companies where it can cost as much as £1000 per employee for companies of up to five people, but only £200 per employee for companies with more than 100 workers.

Consequence of Red Tape: The findings from the World Bank are clear - where the regulatory burden is highest so the black economy is the most active. This not only reduces the amount of taxes paid to the government, but also discourages companies from expanding and increasing their workforce. This should be an incentive for Governments to be more hospitable to small businesses (see my book on the *Small Business Entrepreneur* for more discussion on red tape and the black market).

Exercises:

1. Discuss how your company is using technology products that have only been introduced in the past five to ten years.
2. Discuss how you are using new technology products at home that have only been introduced in the past five to ten years.
3. Discuss how and why large companies are outsourcing their non-core activities to small entrepreneurial companies.

Instructor's Manual: An Instructor's Manual is available with additional exercises and case studies, see *<www.knowledgezone.net>*.

4
Who Wants To Be An Entrepreneur?

LEARNING OUTCOMES - enables the reader to:

Describe how the staircase to wealth outlines a career path for the entrepreneur to follow.

Outline how the entrepreneur benefits from identifying employment triggers and blocks.

Explain how lifestyle entrepreneurs strive to create a balance between earning mega bucks and quality of life.

Discuss how young people, the over 50s and retirees can find effective employment by using entrepreneurial techniques.

"*Who wants to be a millionaire?*", is a popular TV programme that captures our imagination. We clearly associate wealth with happiness. More wealth equals more happiness. Wealth gives us a big house, a quality car, holidays in the sun and no financial worries.

However, most of us probably think we do not have the remotest chance of becoming a millionaire - or do we? At the last count Britain boasted 7,000 millionaires and counting. What is their secret?

This chapter will discuss how the staircase to wealth can outline a career path for the entrepreneur to follow to give them the greatest earning potential. This is followed by a section on triggers and blocks - entrepreneurs need to be able to identify employment triggers which help them become entrepreneurs, and also identify the blocks which might prevent them becoming entrepreneurs.

Entrepreneurs come in all shapes and sizes - there is not one caps fits all. This chapter will also discuss how the entrepreneurial approach can be used effectively by all sectors of our society.

1. Staircase To Wealth

The **staircase to wealth** (figure 4.1) outlines an interesting approach for the entrepreneur to create wealth. Starting at the bottom of the staircase, people working for a salary or self-employed cannot earn any more than their labour rate, they can only gain leverage from education and promotion. However, owners of companies can step up the staircase because they can gain leverage by earning a share of their employees' labour rate - the more employees, the more income.

Manufacturers are on the next step up because they can gain leverage by earning a percentage markup on their products - the more products they sell the more income. Investors are on the next step up because they can gain leverage by investing in rapid growth ventures - the greater the expansion of the venture the more income.

Entrepreneurs are at the top of the staircase because they are the new venture and market makers. It is the entrepreneur who spots the business opportunity in the first place, and then co-ordinates the resources to make-it-happen. (see my book on *Small Business Entrepreneur* for a chapter on the staircase to wealth).

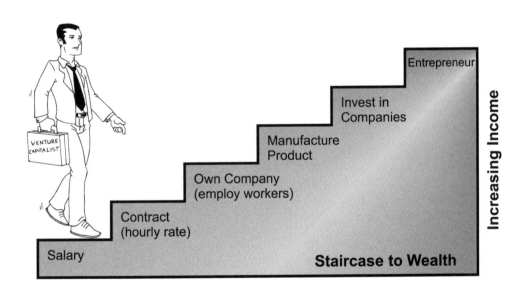

Figure 4.1: Entrepreneur's Staircase to Wealth

2. Triggers and Blocks

Making the transition from secure employment to uncertain self-employment is a brave and courageous decision which all entrepreneurs need to make at some point. This transition is often prompted by a **trigger** which kick-starts the entrepreneur into action.

A trigger may be defined as the stimulus to make the change and can be subdivided into push and pull factors. A push factor is a trigger that forces and kicks a person out of their present job into self-employment, for example, becoming unemployed and need to find a job to pay the bills. While a pull factor is a trigger that encourages and attracts a person to leave their present employment to pursue something they perceive as better, for example, to develop a hobby or marketable opportunity using the latest technology.

Push Factors: The following triggers may force and kick a person into becoming a 'necessity' entrepreneur:

- unemployment, redundancy or retirement - in each case the person needs to work for an income
- an argument with the boss
- interpersonal conflict with another team member
- a disability, illness or accident which makes it difficult for the person to perform their current job
- the loss of a licence which is needed in order to carry out the work, such as a driving licence, medical licence, or legal licence.

Any of these situations could be the push factor that forces someone to become an entrepreneur. The entrepreneurial approach is to consider self-employment by setting up a small business.

Pull Factors: The following triggers encourage and attract employees to leave their present jobs and use entrepreneurial skills to pursue an area of interest, hobby or passion:

- a desire for a more meaningful lifestyle - becoming entrepreneurial enables the entrepreneur to turn their hobby and interests into a lifestyle business
- a desire to be independent, to be 'your own boss' and feel in control of your own destiny. The entrepreneur will still have to network of course, but now they are doing this for their own benefit
- to feel a sense of achievement from their work - a feeling of a job well done
- to receive recognition for their work, and be acknowledged for doing a good job

- feeling frustrated that their creative ability is being stifled, not receiving support or encouragement from their boss - working in their own business will enable them to experiment with new ideas and opportunities
- feel their personal development is being restricted by their boss and company - working in their own business will enable them to pursue their best career path
- to increase the prospect of personal wealth by setting up a small business and climbing up the staircase to wealth (figure 4.1).

Research indicates that, although push factors may be good at forcing someone to become an entrepreneur and start a business, it is the pull factors that have a better track record of business success. This is because the push factors are usually a knee-jerk reaction to leave the company, whereas the pull factors are a driving ambition to do something better and more interesting. The pull factor is also a more considered transition, with time for proper planning, implementing and control.

Blocks: Blocks are the opposite to triggers. A block puts obstacles in the entrepreneur's path making it difficult to set up a venture. The main self-employment blocks are:

- a need for regular income to support a family and pay the monthly bills and mortgage
- a lack of capital and financial support to fund a new venture - without funds the entrepreneur cannot buy material and market his product
- a lack of self-confidence and doubts about their own ability to pursue an entrepreneurial venture
- a lack of courage to take the first step to entrepreneurship.

The underlying cause of these blocks is lack of confidence in one's own ability and being unable to accept the risk of self-employment.

Push   Pull   Block   Pot of Gold

3. Lifestyle Entrepreneurs

An increasing number of people are trying to strike a balance between earning mega-bucks in the city and having a meaningful lifestyle - perhaps in the country. They feel that earning a large salary is not an end in itself and are looking for a more balanced and enjoyable lifestyle.

These people use their entrepreneurial skills to set up a lifestyle company to provide an adequate income for a comfortable middle class way of life. Examples of lifestyle companies would include a person who enjoys playing golf opens a golf pro shop, a person who enjoys cooking opens a restaurant, and a person who enjoys working on cars opens a garage.

A lifestyle company will typically stay small and independent. It will depend heavily on its founders, and grow incrementally as internal funds become available. Ploughing the profits back into the business is called sustainable growth (see the chapter on *Managing Growth* for more discussion on lifestyle companies).

".....buy the Vodafone shares...."

4. Young Entrepreneurs

Gone are the days when a good education and a CV guaranteed the school leaver a job. In today's competitive market, employers are looking for young people with not only excellent qualifications but also appropriate work experience.

This is a classic '*catch 22*' situation – where the school leavers cannot get a job without appropriate work experience, and they cannot get work experience without a job. How can they get out of this closed loop? The young person starting his career must think the world has gone crazy. Is this situation a trigger or a block?

It is actually a combination of both. It is a common employment block, which triggers young people into using entrepreneurial techniques and lateral thinking to overcome the block. It would appear that not only can young people become effective entrepreneurs, but for many of them it is essential to become entrepreneurial to secure rewarding employment.

To gain appropriate work experience the young entrepreneur should consider looking for ways to get a foot in the door even if it means taking on seemingly mundane jobs to build up their work experience. They should look at jobs, not as a position, but for the type of work involved and experience gained. Employers want to see that not only are their employees responsible and honest, but that they can also interact with customers, handle money, negotiate a deal, control stock (JIT), work to standards, understand health and safety requirements, handle dangerous goods and give good customer service.

Michael Dell: Some young entrepreneurs cannot wait to leave school to become millionaires. A good example is Michael Dell who started his computer business from his dormitory room at the University of Texas. Dell was a whiz kid who focused on building better computers and selling them directly to the customer for less than the established computer manufacturer's price. Dell's entrepreneurial approach integrates manufacturing with the demand, and cuts out the middleman by dealing directly with the customer through broad based advertising and B2B (business-to-business) and B2C (business-to-customer) procurement.

5. Female Entrepreneurs

Statistics suggest that female entrepreneurs are more successful than male entrepreneurs. Men typically begin their first business enterprise between 25-35, while women start a little later between 30-40 and are more likely to be better qualified (with diplomas and degrees). Women and men are driven by different needs - women are driven by a need for security, financial autonomy and self-fulfilment, while men are motivated by their ego and the challenge of a new venture.

Women tend to use less start up capital than men, and tend to use known technology and established markets - they are therefore less of a risk taker. This more conservative approach may be because women are typically necessity entrepreneurs - for example, they need to become an entrepreneur to feed the family and pay the bills.

6. Over 50 Entrepreneurs

As people get older and more experienced they generally move up the career ladder which, ironically, rather than making their jobs more secure, in some cases actually highlights them as first on the list for '*the chop*' when the company needs to cut back.

I have already discussed how young people are initially rejected because they do not have any experience. Now we have almost the opposite situation where the over 50s are often rejected because they have too much experience! The over 50s may be out of work for many reasons. The company may be:

- downsizing
- restructuring
- retreating to core activities
- installing new technology
- installing automated production lines.

Even with an expanding workforce, companies may still want to off load older workers because, on average, they cost the company more in pensions and health care, and are also less likely to introduce new ideas in a competitive economy.

Statistics confirm that when the over 50s become unemployed they have great difficulty getting back into the workforce. This is not only a waste of fully qualified and experienced resources, but a sad way to finish one's career, leaving these unemployed people feeling unwanted, with low morale and low self-esteem.

They must feel as if they have been thrown on the scrap heap and have the further indignity of becoming a financial burden on the state. The challenge is to get these over 50s back into the workforce not only contributing to the economy, but also living a meaningful life.

Entrepreneurial Approach: After a person has applied for numerous jobs and has not been called to any interviews it would seem obvious they have hit an employment block. The block, in this case, is the perception by many employers that people over 50 are too old. The trigger (push) is to use entrepreneurial techniques to explore ways of getting around the block. Consider the following entrepreneurial tactics:

- **Direct Marketing:** The entrepreneurial approach is to make a list of companies they might be able to work for and contact them directly. Only one in five jobs are advertised outside a company so this should improve their chances.
- **Trade Jobs:** As a person's career progresses up the career ladder, so they tend to move off their '*tools*' to supervisory and managerial positions. Trade jobs are usually easier to find, so the entrepreneurial approach is to consider going back on the '*tools*'.
- **Contract Work:** Instead of looking for full time employment with all the associated commitments for the employer, the entrepreneurial approach is to present themselves as a self-employed person, or a company looking for a short-term contract.
- **Product:** The entrepreneurial approach is to repackage themselves as a product, for example, instead of applying for lecturing positions, the entrepreneur could sell training courses directly to the students.
- **Networking:** When the entrepreneur needs a job, this is the time to call in favours from people who '*owe you one*'. This is where networking over the years will pay dividends (see *Networking* chapter).
- **Training:** To be employable a person has to have the latest skills. If the economy is in recession the entrepreneurial approach is to consider studying to up-skill to be in a better position to make the most of the next upturn in the economy and catch the wave.

In the UK, the NatWest bank has reported that the number of people becoming entrepreneurs over the age of 45 is increasing, and the average age of people starting their own business has increased to 39 years old.

Research from Warwick University found that in Britain 70% of the new businesses started by people over 50, survived more than three years; while only 30% of companies started by 25 year olds survived more than three years - so maybe older people do make more successful entrepreneurs!

7. Senior Entrepreneurs

In 1889, when Germany's Otto von Bismarck suggested that the state should look after the elderly he greatly reduced the poverty of older people. Pay-as-you-go pensions worked well while the active workforce vastly outnumbered the retirees. The retirement age then was 70, and the life expectancy was only 48. Now the retirement age has reduced to 65, but life expectancy has increased to over 75.

There are three trends running in parallel which are compounding the retirement situation - or perhaps creating an entrepreneurial opportunity:

1. There is a bulge in retirement numbers caused by the post war baby boomers.
2. There are more people in retirement due to higher life expectancy and, further, early retirement means people are living longer in retirement.
3. There are less people working due to: a fall in fertility rates (birth rates after the Second World War have fallen from 2.7 to 1.5 per family); automation of production lines; and outsourcing work offshore.

This is supported by the fact that the work force in the UK is shrinking for the first time since the Black Death! This means more people need support for longer, and there are increasingly going to be less and less people working to support them - clearly an unsustainable situation. In this giant pyramid scheme, the government's payment to pensions is approaching high levels, so governments are going to have to do something drastic to address the imbalance before the pyramid becomes top heavy. There are two main options:

• extend the retirement age
• reduce pension benefits

Either way pensioners are going to have to become more entrepreneurial and look after themselves financially. In America the trend has already started as one in four pensioners are going back to work because they cannot survive on their retirement income.

8. Immigrant Entrepreneurs

Research shows that when immigrants arrive in a new country they often go straight into self-employment and entrepreneurship. This may be partly caused by a resistance to employ immigrants - a clear employment block. When an expat is taken out of his home environment, surviving the hardships and employment blocks often leads to innovation and enterprise. The very experience of surviving in a foreign country encourages qualities of self-restraint, abstinence, hard work and entrepreneurship.

Starting up a business in a new country is not easy for immigrants, but this is another factor which motivates them to work long hours to make a go of their new life. With limited options open to them, they have little to lose from failure and much to gain from success.

Exercises:

1. Research shows that 80% of entrepreneurs start their first venture in the field of their training and expertise. Consider your own training and experience and identify a number of possible enterprise opportunities.

2. The successful dot coms made their investors rich because they were able to target a large potential client base. Develop a dot com type business product which could have a wide international appeal.

3. Select a millionaire businessman who has made it and develop a proposal for a similar type of business in your location.

Instructor's Manual: An Instructor's Manual is available with additional exercises and case studies, see *<www.knowledgezone.net>*.

5
Entrepreneur Traits

LEARNING OUTCOMES - enables the reader to:

Outline how entrepreneurs can be subdivided into a number of different types relating to their personality and traits.

Discuss how a person's upbringing can influence their entrepreneurial traits.

Discuss how entrepreneurs turn the need for formal education on its head.

Highlight a number of undesirable entrepreneurial traits.

Have you had a difficult childhood - been bullied at school, can't spell, can't add up? If this sounds familiar, then you could have had the perfect background to be an entrepreneur!

Would you be able to recognise an entrepreneur if you met one in the street? According to research, if you know what to look for, the entrepreneurs' actions, behaviour and traits could give them away. So by identifying these traits, maybe we can use them as role models to help us get started and become entrepreneurs ourselves!

An entrepreneur's traits could be defined as their natural way of doing things; their natural approach to tackling problems, their natural way of searching for opportunities, their ability to network with their contacts, and their willingness to accept risks. By looking at the entrepreneur's traits we can build up a picture, a sort of 'identikit' of an entrepreneur's likely characteristics and behaviour.

Spot the entrepreneur!

1. Types of Entrepreneurs

Although entrepreneurs have been around since the year dot, as a management science, entrepreneurship is relatively new. Consequently there is still plenty of discussion about '*what are*' the key entrepreneurial traits. Some of the traits discussed in this chapter might appear to be contradictory simply, because there is no one type of entrepreneur but a range of entrepreneur types who might approach the management of their businesses in very different and diverse ways.

In Britain entrepreneurs used to be stereotyped as racketeers and spivs - Arthur Daley (from *Minder*) and Dell Boy (from *Only Fools and Horses*) would have been considered typical entrepreneurs - opportunists who thrive in a world of dodgy deals, and hoodwink their customers into parting with their money. This has changed. The media now presents entrepreneurs as professional business people, such as Richard Branson and Anita Roddick, who are searching for innovative opportunities to drive their businesses.

The *Times* newspaper recently published an article which subdivided entrepreneurs into four types:

- '*Social entrepreneurs who enter business to make the world a better place.*' [rare].

- '*Status entrepreneurs who are driven to reach the top of their field.*' [sounds familiar].

- '*Power entrepreneurs who need to have money to buy the lifestyle they want.*' [sounds logical].

- '*Revenge entrepreneurs who have often been marginalised in childhood or work and strive to put it right.*' [surprisingly common].

A recent *BBC* programme on millionaires subdivided entrepreneurs into three distinct types:

- '*Social entrepreneurs who are driven by the desire to improve society.*' For example, William Booth founded the Salvation Army which looks after the homeless.

- '*Theme entrepreneurs who start a business within a defined area.*' For example, Anita Roddick opened the *Body Shop* in the area of natural beauty products.

- '*Serial entrepreneurs who look for opportunities to create wealth anywhere and everywhere, will set up one company after another in quick succession.*' For example, Richard Branson (*Virgin Group*) has an airline, credit card service, mobile phone service and a soft drinks company. Another serial entrepreneur is Stelios Haji-Iiannou (*easyGroup*) who has an airline, Internet cafes, cinemas and a car hire company.

All these types of entrepreneurs are motivated by one of three factors - status, power and revenge. And the roots of that stem overwhelmingly from their childhood experiences. As the BBC documentary explains:

- '*Status entrepreneurs are driven to create a situation where they are highly respected by the people they think matter. Something in their childhood has made them feel excluded and they are determined to show the world that they fit in.*'

- '*Power entrepreneurs are driven by the desire to show people they can do whatever they want to do. What drives all of them is the desire to create wealth to appease their feelings of insecurity. It is not about money, it is about providing security from slipping back into their previous existence.*'

- '*Revenge entrepreneurs are driven to put right a social injustice to their family or to themselves, which they experienced as a child.*'

2. Are Entrepreneurs Born or Made?

Are entrepreneurs born or made? There is some evidence to suggest that genetics can contribute to a person's personality but, what appears to be more important, is how a young person's genetic make-up is cultivated. How is their development encouraged or discouraged in their early years? Human beings are designed to learn and experiment - no one has to teach a child to walk and talk. Children are fully equipped with an insatiable drive to explore and test. Unfortunately, as children grow up, their natural curiosity and impulse to learn is often curtailed by their parents and teachers.

Family Link: Researchers have found a link between the entrepreneur and his family. If the father was an entrepreneur then his children are more likely to follow in his footsteps and also become entrepreneurs.

Children brought up in the close proximity of their entrepreneurial parents will obviously be influenced by the small business working environment. The '*table talk*' would establish entrepreneurial norms and expectations. The children would see their parents making and promoting their products and would probably be asked to help in the business from time to time - all hands to the pumps.

Anita Roddick, founder of the Body Shop, attributes some of her success to her difficult childhood. Her father died when she was 10 and her mother owned a café. "*There are all these senses of loss that come with an entrepreneur. For me it was the loss of my father - [I was] pushed into being much more responsible. We had no money - so you have to think really creatively about how you survive.*"

The family link can also have negative connotations. The saying goes '*One generation makes the wealth, the next generation spends it, and the following generation loses it*' - from shirt sleeves to shirt sleeves in three generations.

"*.... sorry can't wait to make my first million...*"

3. Are Entrepreneurs Intelligent?

Entrepreneurs who have innovative ideas are usually thought of as being highly intelligent. Their ability to come up with creative ideas is thought of as something special - and special equals intelligence. Intelligence is usually measured with an IQ test. The findings from Stanford University suggest that a certain level of IQ is necessary to be innovative but, interestingly, scores above 120 do not imply greater creativity.

People with a high IQ are good at focusing on a problem and coming up with the solution very quickly, whereas creative people tend to come up with a variety of solutions simultaneously. It has been suggested that people with a high IQ use a small area of their brain very efficiently, whereas creative people co-ordinate several regions of their brain to produce a flood of ideas.

Entrepreneurs have turned the importance of **education** on its head. Research shows entrepreneurs are typically not academic achievers! Far from it; they are often only average or below average! In fact a disproportionate number of entrepreneurs are actually dyslexic which almost certainly holds them back at school. Surprisingly, this could indicate that education is not an entrepreneurial requirement, and might actually be a hindrance. Too much education might actually suppress the entrepreneurial talent we are looking for!

However, if entrepreneurs want to enter a technology driven business, for example, computing, aerospace, or nanotechnology, they will definitely benefit from a technical education because, without an understanding of the new technology, they will not be able to make sound business decisions even though they might be streetwise.

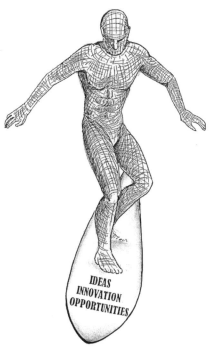

It is generally accepted that the tools and techniques of entrepreneurship (and leadership) can be taught and learned. But it is that inexplicable 'X' factor that makes all the difference – the drive, the self-confidence, the persistence, the passion and the risk taking. There is compelling evidence to suggest that certain negative factors such as dyslexia and being bullied at school, actually create a very strong positive drive and a determination to succeed.

"....I'm surfing for opportunities...."

4. Dyslexic

Who would have thought that being dyslexic would help the entrepreneur become a millionaire? Well, it is true. A study by the BBC has revealed that millionaires are significantly more likely to suffer from dyslexia than the rest of the population. Psychologists who analysed the mental make-up of business winners found learning difficulties seemed to be an important precursor to financial success. About 40% of those studied had been diagnosed with dyslexia — four times the national average!

Experts believe one reason may be that dyslexics, who tend not to be good at details, learn to excel by **grasping the bigger picture.** They do not waste time analysing the detail and are therefore able to make decisions much quicker. They might also be more motivated to achieve because of their social exclusion at school. The findings show that a huge majority of Britain's estimated 7,000 self-made millionaires performed badly at school and continue to perform poorly in aptitude tests today, even though they are raking in the profits.

Sir Richard Branson, head of the Virgin Group, who made his first million by the age of 18 after founding a record label, is a classic example of a successful person with dyslexia. Branson, now a billionaire, admits he did not understand the difference between net profit and gross profit until it was explained to him only a few years ago. *"One of the problems about being dyslexic is that you don't perform well at school and I knew I wasn't going to pass my exams so I did other things,"* said Branson. *"Being dyslexic means I am good at delegation and looking at the bigger picture."*

Jamie Oliver, *'the Naked Chef';* is another dyslexic who has done extraordinarily well. To get around his reading and writing limitations Jamie records the recipes for his TV shows and books on a dictaphone for others to transcribe. Jamie had a tough time at school. He said he was teased for being in the *'special needs class'*. He said his dyslexia was the driving force behind his success. *"It's the* 'nothing-to-lose' *syndrome - the fact that you are so miserably neglected by the education system".*

5. Getting Started

This section will focus on a number of the key traits entrepreneurs use to get new ventures started:

- spotting opportunities
- innovation
- problem-solving
- decision-making
- marketing
- vision.

Spotting Opportunities: Entrepreneurs have a natural ability for spotting opportunities other people only see in hindsight. Entrepreneurs can work in an environment of chaos and ambiguity and piece together a jigsaw of seemingly unrelated snippets of information to help determine which opportunities are worth pursuing. Entrepreneurs start the entrepreneurial process by habitually looking for opportunities or problems to solve so they can offer the market a new product or service.

Successful entrepreneurs are often said to be *'lucky'*. Entrepreneurs accept there are occasions when they are lucky to be in the right place at the right time. For instance being upgraded to first class and then finding themselves sitting beside a potential customer. But what happens next is not luck - the successful pursuit of a lucky opportunity is entirely up to the entrepreneur's proactive networking skills.

Business success does not happen by accident or by luck. It is achieved by those who understand how to recognise opportunities and convert them into profitable realities. Spotting changes in the marketplace means not only detecting trends but also interpreting the impact these changes have on consumer spending. Entrepreneurs are proactive rather than reactive and will actively go looking for opportunities, rather than sit back and wait for lady luck to deliver.

Innovation: Innovation is one of the prime tools entrepreneurs use to create new marketable products. Entrepreneurs are good at adapting and combining existing technology to produce new products to exploit a marketable opportunity. For example, Trevor Baylis' windup radio combined a radio, a rechargeable battery, and a dynamo, to make a windup radio for Africans who could not afford to buy new batteries.

Problem-Solving: Entrepreneurs innovate to overcome problems and obstacles that would put the rest of us off. They have the intrinsic ability to turn problems into opportunities. Entrepreneurs willingly accept the challenge, and are always looking for innovative solutions. Anita Roddick: "*If you sense a problem - you have just found another opportunity*".

Decision-Making: Entrepreneurs will always be the first to step forward and make the decision to get the ball rolling. They take a proactive view to making-it-happen and are experts at articulating their vision. In the face of risk and uncertainty entrepreneurs have the self-confidence and courage to make the decision to start a new venture or enterprise.

Entrepreneurs identify opportunities, create ideas and decide on their actions on the basis of a mixture of rational analysis and **intuition**. The intuitive element of this decision-making process is crucial because it capitalises on the entrepreneur's incredible ability to sift through information and relate situations to their full knowledge base and, most importantly, to every one of their previous experiences. The broader and more relevant their experiences, the more likely their intuitive decisions will lead to positive results.

Marketing: Entrepreneurs are good at understanding their customers' needs, know what their customers will buy and what they are prepared to pay. This enables entrepreneurs to identify new products, new methods of production, and new ways of marketing their products.

Entrepreneurs are eager to engage their customers and encourage them to come back, and next time bring their family and friends. They intuitively know that referrals and return business are the cheapest form of marketing. Entrepreneurs particularly want to find out why a sale is won or lost, because they are willing and able to respond to what the customer is telling them.

Vision: Entrepreneurs are good at imposing their vision on the world. Steve Jobs convinced the world of his vision of having a computer on every desk. No market research at the time would have given the PC the slightest chance of success. Which is why, in the late 70s, so many '*well managed*' computer companies turned down the opportunity to make the desktop and left it to small companies, such as Apple Computers, to pioneer the desktop and enable Apple to be the first to get their foot in the market.

6. Make-It-Happen

Once a course of action has been decided the entrepreneur has the self-confidence and drive to make the new venture happen. While everyone is looking around for direction and support - the entrepreneur is on the phone networking.

Entrepreneurs are driven by a strong inner urge to get things done and succeed - they are not procrastinators. Starting a new venture can be a lonely affair, without outside motivation and encouragement. The entrepreneur often has to work long hours, sometimes with little reward. It is at these times the entrepreneur needs the following traits:

- determination
- persistence
- passion.

Determination: When entrepreneurs buy into a new venture, they are usually fully committed '*lock stock and barrel*'. They are like a '*bull at a gate*'; they are determined '*as the terminator*' to make the venture succeed and will tackle any problem head on. Diplomacy is not one of their strong points.

Persistence: Entrepreneurs do not give up at the first hurdle. In fact they see problems and failures as a challenge. If things do not go the way they want, they do not take no for an answer. They are persistent, tenacious, obstinate and will try again and again until they get what they want (do you remember Robert the Bruce's spider?).

Passion: Entrepreneurs are passionate about their product - a passion which drives them to constantly improve their product until it is right for the market. Entrepreneurs are always thinking about their product and the market potential, looking for opportunities to improve the product's design and gain competitive advantage. Without this driving passion lesser mortals would soon lose interest.

A **cobbler** once told me about the passion he had for designing shoes. He would start with the idea for a new shoe, make a sketch of the shoe, then make a prototype of the shoe. He would then take the shoe with him everywhere he

"....I've got this great idea for a shoe...."

went and keep thinking about the shoe until he got it right. He would have it on the table at dinner; he would have it beside his bed at night; he would go to sleep thinking about the shoe and wake up in the morning with some new ideas. Eventually, he would converge on an optimum design. Today he has a thriving shoe business!

7. Timing is Everything

Entrepreneurs love a challenge - and beating their competitors to market with a new product gives them enormous satisfaction. Entrepreneurs know they have to move quickly while their ideas still have currency - opportunities do not wait forever.

In a competitive market entrepreneurs need to be able to balance the speed of execution with the quality of the product. Entrepreneurs are smart enough not to produce a shoddy job, but a product that suffices, because they want their customers to come back for more. Entrepreneurs instinctively know repeat business is the cheapest form of marketing.

Small business entrepreneurial companies are active mostly in the initial stages of a developing technology because they can respond quicker to innovative opportunities and are more flexible than large bureaucratic corporations. But, as the technology stabilizes, so the large corporations build large manufacturing plants which achieve an economy of scale. In the meantime the entrepreneurs are looking for another niche market. This happened to the small innovative car manufacturers (MG, Lotus and Aston Martin) - one by one they have been taken over by the large multi-national car corporations.

Entrepreneurs hate dealing with **bureaucratic** companies and managers who take a long time to make a decision. Entrepreneurs are impatient and are always looking for ways to cut corners to get the job done as quickly as possible. Because of their 'overview' thinking style, they do not need to conduct an elaborate feasibility study to enable them to make a decision.

Entrepreneurs are frightened off by contracts the size of door stops - they prefer to rely on trust and a handshake. Although they are wheeler-dealers, they are essentially honest. If contracts are needed they like to leave the detailed paperwork to someone else.

Currently, speed is the key competitive advantage. It is not a question of who does it better, it is who gets there first. Time used to be the enemy – now time is the assassin! With increasing wealth and affluence time is replacing money as the essential commodity of life because, once you have sufficient funds, time can never be recovered. It used to be the 'big eat the small', now it is the 'fast eat the slow'.

8. Team Work

The discussion on entrepreneurs working in teams is split into two camps – on the one hand entrepreneurs are thought of as being poor team members who prefer to work alone. On the other hand entrepreneurs are thought of as charismatic leaders who inspire their team members to follow - these two positions are obviously at opposite ends of a continuum.

Forming teams is not always a natural trait for entrepreneurs who are typically egotistical and independent, but if the entrepreneur wants his company to grow, then he must increase the number of team members. If the entrepreneur cannot make the transition from a one-man band to a dynamic team his company will simply reach its natural ceiling quicker and stick there.

There have been many research projects into team dynamics and team composition. I was fortunate to have been involved in Meredith Belbin's research into management teams while I was at Henley Management College. Belbin identified that people working in teams have dual roles - a functional role which relates to the person's area of expertise and a 'team role' which relates to the person's position in the team. The team role may be less obvious than the functional role but when working in teams it might actually be more important.

Belbin identified nine team roles which are required to form a balanced team. Of these nine team roles there are two team roles which seem to fit the entrepreneur's traits quite closely - namely the Resource Investigator and the Shaper.

The **Resource Investigator** specialises in searching for resources outside the team through his network of contacts. The Resource Investigator instinctively knows it is who you know that opens the doors of opportunity. He is able to beg, borrow and befriend, but always gets a good deal on resources which helps the team to achieve competitive advantage.

Through his network of contacts the Resource Investigator will look for solutions to the teams problems to see if someone in another company has already solved the problem - why reinvent the wheel? He will take the teams ideas and test them in the market (informal market research). He will also identify ideas and opportunities in the market and bring them back for the team to consider - this could completely change the teams direction and focus.

The other entrepreneur team role Belbin identified was the **Shaper**. As the name implies, the Shaper influences the shape of the team through his leadership and direction. The Shaper focuses the teams efforts on the job at hand, he sets the objectives and establishes the team's priorities. He clarifies people's roles and contribution within the team. He co-ordinates the team's efforts, monitors their progress, and will intervene to keep the team on track.

9. Undesirable Traits

Unfortunately not all entrepreneurial traits can be considered positive. Some traits are unquestionably undesirable and anti-social which can lead to unpleasant family problems.

Self-Confidence: The down side of an entrepreneur's self-confidence is that it can turn into an exaggerated opinion of his own self-importance leading to arrogance. When the entrepreneur is driving around in a Bentley with all the trappings of wealth it must be hard not to have an exaggerated opinion of oneself.

Low Affiliation: Beware of low affiliation needs and self-reliance as this can result in a distant family life. Spouses and children can be squeezed out by a blend of emotional independence and excessive working hours (60 plus hours per week is not uncommon).

Poor Concentration and Impatience: Entrepreneurs are often restless and easily bored. They like to rush ahead and get things done and get impatient with bureaucracy. They do not want to wait for companies and people who lag behind. It goes without saying that they do not suffer fools gladly and diplomacy is not one of their strong points.

Poor Listeners: Entrepreneurs are not necessarily great listeners. They like the sound of their own voice, and why waste time listening to other people's advice when they have no intention of taking it!

Rude: Entrepreneurs' social attitudes can raise a few eyebrows - they are the ones talking on a mobile phone at a dinner party. They are not interested in life outside their business activities. They are driven 24/7/365 days of the year to pursue their latest venture, and hate taking holidays which could cut them off from their work.

Exercises:

1. From the Times and BBC articles in this chapter, discuss what type of entrepreneur category best fits your natural approach? How have you displayed these traits?

2. How has your upbringing, family life and schooling influenced and encouraged you to become an entrepreneur?

3. What entrepreneurial traits have you used to start a new venture?

Instructor's Manual: An Instructor's Manual is available with additional exercises and case studies, see <*www.knowledgezone.net*>.

6
Creative
Ideas

LEARNING OUTCOMES - enables the reader to:

Discuss how entrepreneurs use creative thinking and innovation to create a novel solution to a problem.

Discuss how entrepreneurs use lateral thinking to solve problems conventional vertical thinking cannot solve.

Discuss how entrepreneurs spot opportunities.

Discuss how companies formally approach creative thinking and innovation through the R&D department.

Our minds work in mysterious ways – one minute we think logically and rationally, the next minute we think intuitively and laterally. It is the entrepreneurs' ability to vary the way they think that enables them to come up with many of their creative and innovative ideas.

Entrepreneurs have a reputation for being able to spot opportunities other people miss, even though the same information is there for all to see. Entrepreneurs appear to thrive in a climate of ambiguity and chaos - they can sift through large amounts of information, piecing together snippets of seemingly unrelated information until they come up with a potential opportunity. Entrepreneurs can sense by instinct what clues are worth pursuing - they can smell an opportunity.

A good idea for a new venture or small business does not need to be earth shatteringly complicated or high tech. Entrepreneurs have always known the secret is to find a simple way of providing something that is perceived to be better, cheaper or more efficient than the competition.

A definition of creativity and innovation for the entrepreneur must be expressed around their ability to spot marketable opportunities and find profitable ways to supply their niche market customers.

Inventions, creations, innovations and spotting opportunities are the cornerstone of entrepreneurial ventures, so understanding how they evolve and develop is important. However, what precisely constitutes creativity and innovation is often hard to define, because they are often used interchangeably.

For example, Trevor Baylis is acknowledged as the inventor of the windup radio. But he did not invent the radio, he did not invent the rechargeable battery and he did not even invent the dynamo. However, he was the first person to assemble these three components into a workable windup radio with a clear target market in mind - the Africans who could not afford to buy batteries. Trevor also felt the radio was the best means to inform the Africans living outside the cities, about Aids prevention. This venture has been a great success story with over 2 million radios sold.

In producing the windup radio Trevor combined invention and innovation to produce a unique product from a number of commonly used components. By identifying the market, Trevor linked the first two topics on the entrepreneurship spiral. Trevor then joined forces with a funder and a manufacturer to complete the spiral.

1. Creative Thinking

Creative thinking is the use of ingenuity and imagination to create a novel approach or a unique solution to a problem. In the *Do We Really Need Entrepreneurs?* chapter, the need was expressed in the context of companies having to respond to changing technology and changing markets by employing people who are creative, innovative and entrepreneurial.

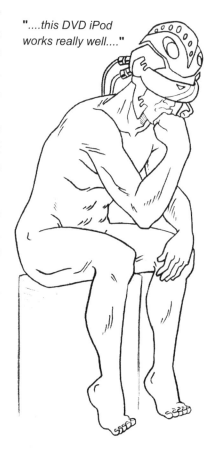

"....this DVD iPod works really well...."

Creative thinking is a mysterious process by which we come up with a stream of creative ideas. At one end of the creative continuum are great advances in science and technology called 'paradigm shifts'. Science is not necessarily a smooth transition of incremental inventions, but rather a series of revolutions, expressed as paradigm shifts. A paradigm means a set of assumptions, methods, and models that define the change.

In Britain, between 1775 to 1825, the canals ushered in the first industrial revolution with a paradigm shift in transportation. More recently, the Internet has created a paradigm shift in the medium of communication, which in turn has facilitated the knowledge wave (see *Catching the Wave* chapter).

In reality very few companies are likely to create a paradigm shift. They are more likely to adopt existing technology to design new products. For instance, the previous example of the windup radio, and the **Sony Walkman**, were both an innovative integration of existing technology.

McDonalds, founded by Ray Kroc, led the way in creating a paradigm shift in the food industry. The hamburger chain brought innovation to the food industry by developing a standardised, high quality hamburger produced by new cooking procedures, and delivered with the speed of just-in-time preparation by meticulously trained staff. The food was presented in disposable space age utensils, in spotlessly clean premises, and all at a bargain price. This type of food and service was completely innovative at the time spawning a new product called the '*fast food industry*'.

Lucozade: The '*healthy living*' paradigm shift encouraged Lucozade to innovatively reposition its product in the market place. Traditionally, Lucozade was a health drink aimed at children and convalescents. Now it is marketed as a trendy energy drink aimed at the young and active.

Mini Cooper: To be truly innovative the entrepreneur has to break out of the mould and do something completely different. New cars are rarely innovative despite what the manufacturer's marketing hype might say. But the Mini Cooper was innovative - because it had a completely different drive transmission configuration. The engine was mounted transversely with front wheel drive - this had never been done before. The Mini Cooper's handling characteristics and charisma are immortalised in the film '*The Italian Job*'.

Creative ideas come any time, anywhere - in the car, in the shower, shaving, ironing, peeling potatoes, washing up, walking the dog, mowing the lawn, waiting for a plane, relaxing on a beach - in fact the last place many managers seem to find inspiration to solve their problems is at their office desk! This is because we get our best ideas when our normal everyday consciousness is side lined. This allows our unconscious mind to spontaneously bring creative ideas to the surface.

For every thousand great ideas we have, unfortunately only a few filter through to form the basis of a successful business enterprise. Some ideas will be impractical, some ideas too obscure, but, the important thing is to keep them coming and make sure they are written down. All too often good ideas are lost in the depths of our memory. You wake up knowing you have solved a problem - but you cannot remember how!

2. Lateral Thinking

Edward de Bono is internationally known for coining the phase '*lateral thinking*' from his highly successful book '*The Use of Lateral Thinking*' (1967). His whole approach to personal development was through intellectual thinking - educating the mind to be creative and innovative as a means of escaping established ideas and perceptions in order to find new ones.

De Bono explains how **vertical thinking** or logical thinking, handed down from the ancient Greeks, is our traditional way of thinking. Vertical thinking proceeds directly from one state of information to another, like building a wall, one brick is placed on top of another. It is a step-by-step procedure such as that used to solve a mathematical problem. Vertical thinking uses continuity; like computer programmes, there is a clear link to get from A to B.

In contrast, **lateral thinking** uses discontinuity to get from A to B and, although the link may be obvious after the event, going forward, vertical thinking might not have been able to make that step. The Oxford Dictionary defines lateral thinking as a '*method of solving problems indirectly or by apparently illogical methods*'.

De Bono says these two thought processes work well together to solve a problem. He suggests starting with the logical vertical way of thinking. If this does not solve the problem, then move on to lateral thinking to restructure the problem and look for lateral ways of solving it.

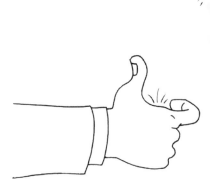

De Bono uses story-telling **humour** to explain how lateral thinking works. In humour the punchline usually reverberates between two hitherto unconnected contexts or frames of reference. This is precisely what happens with insight, which is why we laugh at both the surprise of the punchline (the twist in the tail) and marvel at its ingenuity. There is the humour, where in hindsight the joke makes sense but, in the telling of the story, we are taken along a different line of thinking. It is only in hindsight that we see how narrow, polarized and conditioned our thinking really is.

One of De Bono's favourite stories is about Johnny, who is five years old. He lives in Australia. One day his friends, who want to tease him, offer Johnny a choice of two coins, an Australian $1 coin and the smaller $2 coin. They say, "*Johnny, which one do you want? You can take and keep whichever coin you want.*"

Johnny looks at the coins, his eyes rest on the bigger one and he takes the $1 coin. His friends laugh behind his back and say, "*Isn't Johnny stupid, he doesn't realise that the smaller coin is worth twice the amount of the larger one!*" So, whenever they want to make a fool of him, they offer him the coins and he always takes the bigger one. One day, an adult sees this and calls him over and says, "*Johnny, believe me when I tell you that you are mistaken in taking the larger coin because it is worth half the value of the smaller coin.*" Johnny listens very politely, then says, "*Yes, I know that, but how many times would they have offered it to me if I had taken the smaller coin?*" One has to admit no computer could come up with that logic going forward.

Our life experiences lead us along predictable lines of thinking. This makes it difficult for us to solve new problems because our thought process becomes inflexible, making it difficult to think outside the square. The dominance of this type of thinking suppresses alternative solutions but, by using *lateral thinking* we can produce a rapid succession of different ways of looking at a problem. The dynamic fluidity of lateral thinking is constantly forming, dissolving and re-forming the parts of the situation in ever changing ways, to find the best way of looking at it.

3. Innovation

Innovation is usually perceived as using creative ideas to make a better product, but innovation could also be the substitution of a cheaper material in an existing product, or a better way of marketing, distributing or supporting a product. Innovation is more than a flash of inspiration; it is the systematic development and implementation of the creative idea. Because, if diligence, persistence and commitment are lacking, then talent, ingenuity and knowledge will be self-limited. Innovation is all about '*change*' to improve the product in the eyes of the customer. This could be:

- tailoring the product for a particular need or application
- improving the build-method to reduce manufacturing costs
- streamlining the administration to reduce overheads
- opening a new market, particularly an export market
- finding a new source of material supply, particularly technically superior and cheaper
- improving customer service to encourage repeat business.

A new mobile phone would be a product change, whereas a new method of manufacturing the phone would be a build-method change. A travel agent who combines a flight with accommodation, car hire, and a ticket to a musical concert, would be implementing a service change.

Bird Box: When William's mum was in bed recovering from a hip operation William built her a bird box with a camera so that she could watch the birds in the garden from her bed on her TV. This innovative idea caught on and now William is in full scale production - see <www.cambox.co.uk>. This is an excellent example of how a problem and need created an innovative product which has subsequently developed into a small business opportunity.

From the above discussion it is not surprising that the terms creativity and innovation are often used inter-changeably. But if a distinction is required then creativity focuses on the idea and innovation focuses on the application.

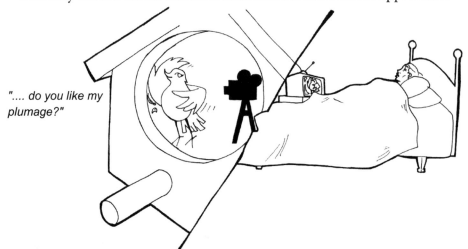

".... do you like my plumage?"

4. Spotting Opportunities

Do you feel gutted when your great ideas are rejected? The Beatles must have felt the same when they were rejected by Decca after their 1962 audition. They were told *"We don't like the sound - guitar groups are on the way out"*.

This has gone down as one of the biggest audition mistakes of all time. Fortunately for the Beatles, George Martin at EMI did recognise their potential and the rest is history. The moral of the story is, entrepreneurs must be confident of their product and have the persistence and determination to keep knocking on doors and believe eventually they will be successful.

Serendipity: Serendipity is the unexpected discovery of a creative idea or solution to a problem. The gift of discovering something by accident while hunting for something else. Inventors and researchers often describe their original discovery as a chance occurrence. For the entrepreneur serendipity and perseverance seem to be linked:

- the harder I work the luckier I get
- the longer I think about a problem the better the solution
- the more time I spend with my customers the more orders I seem to get!

5. R&D

Many companies approach creativity and innovation in a formal way through their R&D (research and development) department. This could be either through an in-house R&D department, or externally through university science parks, or commercial testing facilities. R&D can be subdivided into pure research which investigates new inventions and concepts, or into development which focuses on industrial and commercial applications.

Statistics indicate that companies that spend more on R&D tend to do better because they are able keep up with new technology. This is where large companies have an advantage over small companies, because of the high cost of R&D and the long development times, small companies may not have the cashflow flexibility or be able to afford the lead time between R&D and production. Entrepreneurs working in their garage, for example, are also at a disadvantage compared to development teams who have better facilities, greater depth of knowledge, and team synergy to cross fertilize ideas and solve problems.

Further, large companies are able to spread the risks of innovation over a number of products, whereas a small company may have to put all their eggs in one basket and must get it right each time in order to stay in business. For example, a fashion designer of a small company is unlikely to survive to the next season if they produce a clothing range that does not sell.

Although large companies spend far more on R&D, it is amazing how often the small entrepreneurial companies actually pioneer the introduction of new inventions and radical innovations. However, large companies can always overcome this limitation and remain at the cutting edge, by simply buying out their smaller competitors - this could be considered as a form of R&D outsourcing!

"....I've got a few more bright ideas...."

6. Innovative Companies

Companies need to encourage a climate of creativity, innovation, opportunity-spotting and problem-solving to keep up with new technology and their competitors.

If a company's products are at the leading edge (mobile phones for example), then innovation has to be central to the company's strategy, because innovation is the only real insurance against competition. There needs to be scope for experimentation within a company, a willingness to make mistakes and most importantly, a willingness to learn from mistakes.

Many senior managers only pay lip service to R&D, saying they want their company to generate new ideas, but then do not support a culture of innovation. R&D has to be top-down motivated and acknowledged as a core competency, with rewards and support for innovation. Staff should be continually encouraged to be creative and test the boundaries.

Innovation can be fostered by providing a culture and an environment that values innovation and experimentation, and removes the blame for mistakes and failures. Steve Jobs encouraged creativity to flourish in the making of the film 'Finding Nemo'. Steve said, *".... It's a matter of not stopping it, more than a matter of fostering it. It's [creativity] already there - it's just that there are a lot of environments that stifle it, want to have control over it."*

Although inventors may initiate new ideas, they do not necessarily make good entrepreneurs because they have different characters and skill sets. While an inventor may be good at inventing creative products, it takes different skills to build an effective team, raise funds and resources, manufacture and distribute, and market the product.

Compare Sir Clive Sinclair, the inventor scientist from Cambridge University, with Alan Sugar, who started as a market trader. Both were competing in the home computer market, Sinclair produced the ZX80 and QL, while Alan Sugar (Amstrad) produced the BBC Acorn micro computer.

Sir Clive got the first part of the entrepreneurial process right with innovative products at an attractive price. But it was reported that he was let down by the outsource companies that manufactured his computers. Poor product quality and stand-off customer service became his downfall in the end. The market perception of his products changed from innovative gadgets to unreliable gimmicks. The final nail in the coffin was the C5 scooter - great idea but it never got traction. In contrast, Alan Sugar (BBC Micro computer), who was in a similar market, paid more attention to the production process and customer service and consequently became the successful market leader in the UK.

To be successful, entrepreneurs do not necessarily have to invent an earth shattering new product; they essentially need to spot a marketable opportunity and supply it to their niche market.

Exercises:

1. Give an example of an innovative product which brings together a number of commonly available components to form a new type of product for an identified market, for example, the windup radio.

2. Give an example of a company or product, such as Lucozade, which has rebranded itself to appeal to a new market.

3. To demonstrate lateral thinking, tell a joke where the punch line has a twist in the tail.

Instructor's Manual: An Instructor's Manual is available with additional exercises and case studies, see *<www.knowledgezone.net>*.

7
Innovation Process

LEARNING OUTCOMES - enables the reader to:
Outline how the innovation process can be presented as a flow chart.
Discuss why 'sleeping on it' can solve problems and produce innovative ideas.
Discuss why we need somewhere special to think.
Outline how feasibility studies can be used to confirm an idea will work in practice, and confirm it has a commercial market.

Being innovative and creative on demand is not always as easy as it sounds. Innovation and creativity are not like a tap which can be turned on and off as required. Our mind often plays cruel tricks on us - letting us down just when we need it.

Authors are renowned for getting '*writer's block*' when they cannot put pen to paper. Artists are similarly afflicted by '*paper fright*' when the blank paper is staring them in the face, but no brush strokes are forthcoming. Some students in their crucial final exams get a '*mental block*'. And actors do not escape from these problems either. When they say "*break a leg*" they mean it, because breaking a leg is far preferable to getting '*stage fright*' in front of a packed house.

Although innovation, creativity and problem-solving might ultimately use discontinuous lateral thinking techniques, in practice it is common to present them as a logical process of vertical thinking steps. Consider the following four phase process:

1. **Preparation Phase:** Develop background skills and experience, gather information, impressions and concepts that relate to the problem or opportunity. Restructure the problem to ask the right question to get the best solution.

2. **Incubation Phase:** Let the subconscious sort and re-arrange information - sleep on it.

3. **Inspiration Phase:** Start with the sudden recognition of a solution - Eureka, a flash of inspiration, the emergence of a new and novel solution.

4. **Evaluation Phase:** Compare the new ideas against existing theory, concepts, frameworks and benchmarks. Model test the prototype to ensure the product works. Confirm the new product is an improvement, and identify where refinements and improvements are necessary.

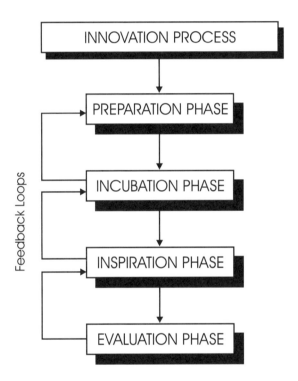

Figure 7.1: Innovation Process - flow chart with successive feedback loops

Although the innovation process is presented here as a simple flow chart, in practice there are many feedback loops between the phases as the entrepreneur strives to create a marketable product.

1. Preparation Phase

The preparation phase of the innovation process is much more extensive than it might first appear, because it includes everything from the entrepreneur's formal education, university of life, to the school of hard knocks, professional skills and work experience. For this reason the entrepreneur is more likely to see an opportunity or solve a problem in his field of expertise. Which means the budding entrepreneur might not appreciate that the subjects they studied at school could greatly influence their subsequent career path.

The solution to a problem is directly influenced by asking the right question. It is therefore important to spend time in the preparation phase to define and redefine the problem to ensure the right questions are being asked to get the best solutions. This should stop the entrepreneur looking for a quick fix by running with their first impressions.

In the preparation phase the entrepreneur should gather information about the problem from all available sources. This should include information from other people who might also have experienced the same problem - and have solved it! This should prevent the entrepreneur trying to reinvent the wheel.

The discovery of the wonder drug **penicillin** in 1928, is a good example of how the preparation phase helped an observant scientist. While **Fleming** had been away on holiday from his laboratory at St Mary's Hospital Medical School in London, a petri dish containing staphylococcus bacteria had become contaminated by a fungal spore. Fleming's educated awareness and alert mind stopped him throwing away the petri dish when he noticed a zone around the fungus was completely devoid of bacteria. Fleming correctly reasoned that this growing fungus must be producing a substance which killed the bacteria. This great medical breakthrough led to the development of penicillin.

It is interesting to note that this preparation phase is missing from **brainstorming** - a widely used problem-solving technique. The technique was first introduced by Alex Osborn in 1938 as a way of removing inhibition and generating ideas. Brainstorming starts with the leader focusing the group on the purpose of the session, outlining the rules of brainstorming, and explaining the background to the problem to be brainstormed. This technique works by the team generating lots of innovative ideas. The best ideas are often from immediate responses to other peoples ideas - but there must be no evaluation as this will kill any further ideas. The ideas are written up on a white board for all to see, which further helps the cross-fertilizing process.

2. Incubation Phase

The incubation phase is the art of letting go; the art of letting your involuntary processes search unconstrained through the mass of unconnected items of information whirling around in your head. You are not going to have a novel idea if you think along structured vertical thinking lines. See lateral thinking in the *Creative Thinking* chapter.

If you cannot solve a problem, consider sleeping on it. Let your subconscious mind do the work undisturbed. When you have gathered information and set out what you want to achieve, it is amazing how the subconscious mind has the capacity to juggle, collate, reinforce and make numerous unconnected links. And when you wake up – voila - surprisingly, you have solved the problem. Even after a short power-nap you can wake up with new creative ideas.

How does it work? This subconscious problem-solving ability is called **hypnagogia** (also called active imagination). Hypnagogia is a word of Greek origin from the same family as hypnosis. It is used to explain a state of deeply relaxed consciousness, between sleep and waking up, during which flashes of inspiration and creative insight often appear. Researchers have found these transition periods to be quite short, seldom more than ten minutes.

When we are awake our attention tends to be narrowly focused and our range of awareness is likely to be relatively constricted. In contrast, when we are in a low arousal state or incubation, our attention is likely to be wider and more diffused. This is when a wide variety of irrelevant cues are more likely to be simultaneously accessible to our awareness. By bringing supposedly irrelevant cues together in our stream of thought, a **vital link** to a new perception of a problem might be provided. In other words, lowering our arousal makes us more open to simultaneous perception and association of hitherto unrelated items.

This way of thinking is precisely the opposite to the traditional educational model of analytical thinking with logic paths and learning by heuristics. Consequently we learn to do things in the narrow plane of our experience, based on the subjective probability that this will reduce risk.

By contrast, active imagination is possible when we move to the threshold between our everyday awareness and the dream world. If we can bring a degree of alertness and openness to this threshold, the dream world will reach out to meet us. The dream world can provide us with its unique view of the world to which we can bring our questions and problems.

Dreams give us an inner freedom to make all sorts of random connections between different items of information. It is like shaking a kaleidoscope of creative ideas which land forming random patterns. Make sure you have a notebook handy to jot down the new ideas as you might not make the same associations again.

Einstein, the great philosopher himself, is said to have had his first insight into relativity as he got out of bed to have breakfast. The hypnagogia theory would suggest this happened while he was waking up, during the transition period from his dream world to a nuclear reality.

3. Inspiration Phase

The inspiration phase sometimes starts with a jolt - **Aha!** - the sudden recognition of a new idea that works. Or it might be only the quick flash of an idea - just like sunlight catching a reef fish - an association which requires more thought to add another piece of information to the jigsaw.

As discussed in the previous chapter, it is common to have these flashes of inspiration anytime, anywhere. This is because our best ideas occur when our normal everyday consciousness is sidelined. This allows our unconscious mind to spontaneously bring things up to the surface.

Retracing thinking steps is easy for the analytical thinker who has followed a structured vertical thinking path. But for the intuitive thinker, who suddenly arrives at a solution from a number of unrelated associations, they might not be able to retrace their mental steps and explain how they solved the problem.

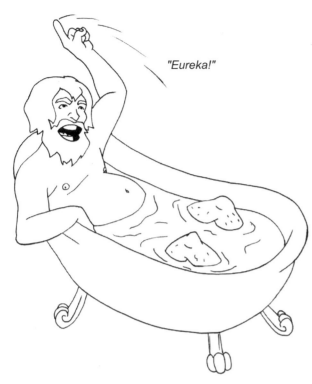

"Eureka!"

An excellent example of the inspiration phase happened to **Archimedes**. As he was relaxing in his bath tub he suddenly discovered the *'principle of flotation'* (that a body floats when it displaces its own weight of water). Shouting out *"Eureka"* Archimedes jumped out of the bath tub and ran naked down the street enthusiastically telling everyone of this astonishing discovery. I can imagine the neighbours were probably more astonished by his appearance!

Sir Isaac Newton experienced a similar flash of inspiration while sitting under an apple tree in the English countryside. As an apple fell from the tree on to Newton's head - Newton suddenly grasped the concept of gravity. He later applied this to the movement of the planets, tides and his famous laws of motion.

Professor Robert Winston's BBC programme *The Human Mind* put these extraordinary historical events into perspective. He showed how a brain trace can reveal an original thought. Robert was wired up to a scanner and given a puzzle to solve. At the exact moment he solved the puzzle **'Aha'** the scanner showed a trace across the screen. This trace indicated an original thought which related directly to the moment of inspiration. Winston stressed that the brain signals are very weak and can easily be lost in the clutter of other brain activity and outside noise.

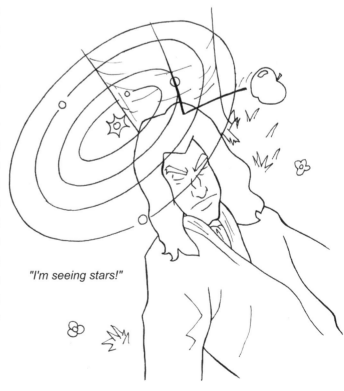

"I'm seeing stars!"

This brain trace helps to explain Newton's moment of inspiration. The apple fell on Newton's head during an 18 month period of exile from London to the Lincolnshire countryside to avoid a bout of the plague. In this relaxed atmosphere, with no interruptions, no distractions, no extraneous clutter – Newton invented calculus, constructed a theory of optics, explained how gravity works and developed most of his famous laws of motion - it was his most productive period (see www. newtonproject.ic.ac.uk).

These examples clearly show how important it is to have somewhere to think and time to think to give the brain waves a chance to establish creative ideas. Entrepreneurs need to find a place where they can relax to think things through - this could be their study, their garage or even their cave!

4. Evaluation Phase

The evaluation phase subjects the entrepreneur's creative ideas and products to thorough evaluation and testing. This can be addressed under the following headings:

- feasibility study
- build-method to confirm the product can be manufactured
- model testing - make a scaled model of the product and conduct a range of tests which can be correlated to full size
- prototype testing - build a full size working prototype of the product and conduct a range of tests
- market research - confirm there is a market and commercial opportunity for the product.

Evaluation can be a challenging time for the entrepreneur. Not only is their product benchmark tested against their competitors and the market expectations, but they might also have to put up with intrusions into their private world - book reviews in my case. It should be acknowledged though that generally we all benefit from feedback and constructive criticism - this helps us grow. A far worse situation would be to have potential customers voting with their feet because they do not like certain features of the product which, with constructive feedback, could easily have been changed.

The selection of the right idea for the right venture for future investment is crucial for the long-term survival of the entrepreneur's company. The selection of the wrong venture might reduce profits and put the entrepreneur's company at risk.

New venture selection is making a commitment for the future. A new venture will tie up the entrepreneur's resources and, as an opportunity cost, the selection of one venture might preclude the entrepreneur from pursuing another venture. We live in a world of finite resources so companies cannot undertake all the ventures they might want or need. Companies therefore require a process to select, rank and prioritise new ventures on the basis of beneficial change to the company (see my book on Project Management, Chapter on *Project Selection*).

Exercises:

1. Discuss how you generate creative ideas.

2. Discuss how your preparation phase has influenced your career path.

3. Does hypnagogia work for you? Outline how you have woken up in the morning with the solution to a problem that has been on your mind the day before.

Instructor's Manual: An Instructor's Manual is available with additional exercises and case studies, see <*www.knowledgezone.net*>.

8
Catching the Wave

Entrepreneurs **catching the wave** might sound a corny phase, but applying this surfing terminology to catching the next wave of opportunity, the next technology wave or the next economic cycle is a sensible innovative way for the entrepreneur to gain competitive advantage. Since the industrial revolution there have been a number of technology waves, each representing a paradigm shift in technology which has encouraged industry to move in a new direction. So if entrepreneurs can identify the next technology wave this will give them time to prepare and position themselves to gain maximum exposure.

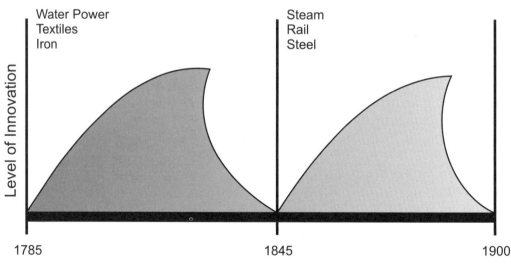

Figure 8.1: Technology Waves

1. Industrial Waves

Since the industrial revolution there has been a number of technology waves which have shaped our environment, society and working lives. The human race seems to adapt very quickly to change, and certainly today's generation takes new technology in their stride. As any historian will tell you, history has a habit of repeating itself - so looking at how the previous waves formed and developed should help us to identify forthcoming waves and prepare for the future.

Figure 9.1 shows five major technology waves which have been driven by different clusters of industry. Economist (February 1999) '*Typically a long upswing in a cycle started when a new set of innovations came into general use - as happened with water power, textiles and iron in the late 18th century; steam, rail and steel in the mid-19th century; and electricity, chemicals and the internal combustion engine at the turn of the 20th century*'.

'*In turn, each upswing stimulated investment and an expansion of the economy. These long booms eventually petered out as the technology matured and returns to investors declined with the dwindling number of opportunities. After a period of much slower expansion came the inevitable decline - only to be followed by a wave of fresh innovations and created the conditions for a new upswing. The **entrepreneurs role** was to act as a ferment in this process of creative destruction, allowing the economy to renew itself and bound onwards and upwards again*'.

These technology waves explain why the American IT industry (5th wave) bounced back in the early 1990s, leaving behind countries which were preoccupied with funding obsolete third and fourth wave industries.

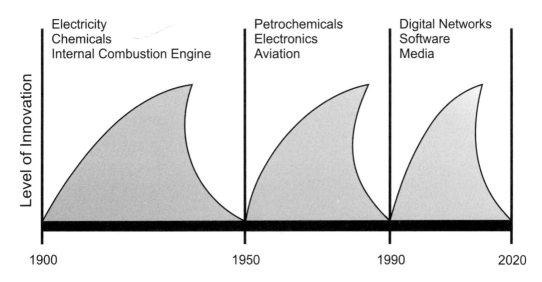

Within a technology wave there will be a number of economic cycles, as supply and demand fluctuates. Just consider how the housing and oil markets move from boom to bust every 10 to 15 years. This is another roller coaster cycle for the entrepreneurs to predict and then position themselves in order to gain maximum exposure.

It is important for entrepreneurs to be aware of forthcoming technology waves and economic cycles, as this indicates the areas of greatest opportunities. If entrepreneurs can catch the wave at the beginning, they will be carried along in a developing and expanding industry - like an incoming tide it will lift all the boats in the harbour. This must be easier than trying to sell products in a declining market where people are tightening their belts to reduce costs.

Entrepreneurs who are experts in their fields will probably do well even in a declining market, but the average entrepreneur will almost certainly do significantly better if they can identify a new technology wave, and get their 'foot in the door' and be carried along with its expansion.

The rate of change in technology is happening more quickly, with ever shortening cycles. We will probably experience a number of technology waves and a number of economic cycles during our life time. Therefore, even if you get the first wave right, you still need to be looking for the next wave to catch.

2. Technology Waves

There are many ways to subdivide technology waves. This section will discuss how four of the key technology waves have developed over the years.

Transport Waves: The world has witnessed a number of transport technology waves which have revolutionised the way we travel and transport goods. It is fascinating to look back on how the pioneering entrepreneurs have revolutionised the transportation systems over the past 200 years from Steptoe's horse and cart to **Brunel's** canals, from Watt's steam engine to Telford's roads, and from Rolls Royce's jet engines to NASA's rockets taking us into the space age.

Power Waves: Power generation has underpinned most industrial changes. The industrial revolution initially started close to a source of power - typically water and coal. Today with the national power grid and large power stations achieving economies of scale (using oil, gas and nuclear fuels), they can be located away from industrial areas. The present trend is to reduce the production of greenhouse gases by using sustainable energy - wind, solar and tidal. Unfortunately all the sources of sustainable energy will not be able to generate sufficient power on their own - the fuel of the future might well be hydrogen extracted from seawater!

Electronic Waves: As electronics have miniaturised from valves and transistors to circuit boards and chips, so computers have become smaller, more powerful and less expensive. It is amazing to think that the notebook computers of today are more powerful than the old IBM mainframes of only a couple of decades ago.

Communication Waves: Microprocessor chips are increasing computer power, and fibre optics and satellites are increasing bandwidths and data transmission speeds - these are all combining to increase international communication facilities. Methods of communication have progressed from post and telegraph, to telephone and fax, and now mobile phone and Internet technology are leading the way. It is now possible for businesses in America, UK, Australia and Hong Kong to speak to each other without considering the cost. The world has suddenly become a much smaller place.

Mobile phone companies and the Internet are the new economic powerhouses driving the economy. They have opened up a whole new platform for communication and doing business. IT facilities have made the mobile office and working from home a feasible option. In fact there are many back office jobs and call centres which are being outsourced and offshored to other countries where the labour rate is more competitive.

Brunel, a 19th century entrepreneur was a key player in the rapid growth of Britain's industrial infrastructure. Pictured here in front of the drag chains of the Great Eastern.

Courtesy of Brunel University Library

3. Knowledge Wave

The developments in computer systems, communications, IT and the Internet have all come together to form the knowledge wave. A knowledge economy is where an increasing number of workers use knowledge and information as their product. In the past we might have traded in manufactured products, but today we can go directly to the Internet and trade information.

As societies have evolved from one type of economy to another, so the skills needed to keep up with the changes have also evolved, together with the education system to support them. In pre-agricultural economies, wealth depended on the availability of resources such as game, fish or fruit and the skill to hunt and catch the food. In agricultural economies, arable land became the primary resource. In industrial economies, raw material and the equipment to transform it into goods became the primary economic resource.

We now live in a knowledge society where an increasing proportion of knowledge workers gain their skills through formal education, particularly tertiary education and short training courses. Their work requires knowledge and information to do the jobs - in fact the education process really never stops. Increasingly an educated person is one who has learnt how to learn and who continually challenges the status of their profession (an entrepreneurial trait). In the new knowledge economy the knowledge worker owns the tools of the product – it is their own education, experience and knowledge.

Knowledge Management involves efficiently connecting those *who know* with those *who need to know*, and converting personal knowledge into organisational

"....the surfs up...."

knowledge. People are wonderful receptacles of valuable ideas and information, but they tend to move on, taking their ideas and information with them. The challenge for companies is to use expert systems to extract and share ideas and information. Thus keeping a knowledge base in the company even after people have left the organisation.

Knowledge is not new, it has always been with us, but what is happening now is a realisation that knowledge is a tangible resource that can be traded as a product.

- Knowledge has become a new currency for business. By adding knowledge to a basic material it is possible to form a knowledge product. For example; software has turned a computer into a fashion design tool; and search engines have turned the Internet into a library of information.
- Knowledge management involves obtaining, distributing and using information so that it flows freely. This includes soliciting ideas from colleagues, customers and other stakeholders.
- For the knowledge process to be effective companies must act on the information and introduce new strategies, change products, and enhance processes and, most importantly, respond to customers' needs, competitors' products, and new technology.

Knowledge and information are frequently confused. Knowledge management is a people issue which is much more complex than managing just pure information. Knowledge management includes the tacit knowledge held inside people's heads, which consists of personal judgments, experiences and values. These qualities cannot be transferred to a central database, although expert systems are making impressive inroads.

Exercises:

1. Identify an industry you are interested in and discuss how technology developments in the past have changed the way products are made and distributed.

2. We are currently in a growing knowledge wave. Discuss how you are using knowledge in your work and your lifestyle, and identify opportunities for future knowledge products.

3. Economic cycles are often caused by politicians delaying infrastructure decisions until they becomes major issues. Discuss how power generation and road building are creating entrepreneurial opportunities in the area where you live.

Instructor's Manual: An Instructor's Manual is available with additional exercises and case studies, see *<www.knowledgezone.net>*.

cosmic mba series

9
Marketing

LEARNING OUTCOMES - enables the reader to:

Know how to conduct market research to determine what the customers want.

Quantify your competition's strengths and weaknesses.

Explain how entrepreneurs achieve competitive advantage by getting their product to market first.

Understand the importance of advertising and promoting your products.

Behind every success story is an innovative product, whether it be an artistic innovation such as Walt Disney's Mickey Mouse, or a technical innovation such as Steve Jobs' Apple computers. But having an innovative product is only half the story - the other half is taking the product to market and selling it. And if the entrepreneur does not take the marketing opportunity by the horns, then their success will be self-limited, and a more proactive entrepreneur will probably seize the opportunity.

This famously happened at Xerox's celebrated Palo Alto Research Centre (PARC) in Silicon Valley, where they were the first company to experiment with many of the computer features we are familiar with today; the fax, mouse, screen icons, graphic user interface (GUI's) and ethernet (the most popular way to distribute data around local networks). However, Xerox's management decided these features were not part of their core business and left them to be successfully developed and exploited by other proactive entrepreneurs - particularly Apple and Microsoft.

The previous chapters on innovation discussed ways to generate creative ideas, spot opportunities, and recognise new technology waves and economic cycles. This chapter will move to the next point on the entrepreneurial spiral (see figure 9.1, repeat of figure 2.2) and discuss how to make the **crucial link between**

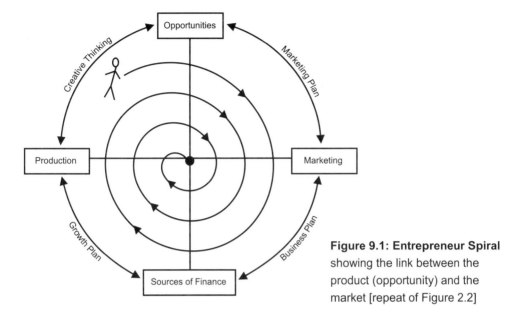

Figure 9.1: Entrepreneur Spiral showing the link between the product (opportunity) and the market [repeat of Figure 2.2]

the product and the market. This is important because, if there is no customer need or market for the brilliant product, then the success will be limited and the entrepreneur will probably be wasting their time, funds and resources.

Inventors are particularly prone to myopic vision when they focus totally on the product's features in complete isolation from the market. Marketing is particularly helpful in keeping the customers central to the product's development.

Marketing is a broad topic; it is much more than just selling the product or service. The market research section below outlines a comprehensive list of areas to consider.

1. Market Research

Market research ensures the entrepreneur is offering the right product to the right people. Basic market research tries to ensure there is a demand for the product and market potential with respect to the competition. There is no point hawking hot dogs when every corner has a hotdog stand. Conversely the entrepreneur might see an opportunity for a better hot dog or even a different type of food (Chinese, Indian, organic or low carb) which they feel will take market share from the competitors.

The commercial objective is usually to sell as much of the product as possible, to optimise the market opportunity and maximise the profits. Consider asking the following questions:

- Can you identify the target market? Can you name one customer who will buy the product? Answering these questions will help to bridge the gap between fantasy and reality.

- What does the market want? Based on this information the entrepreneur might tailor the product and angle the marketing to appeal to the greatest demand. If the product is a completely new idea, such as Apple's iPod, the entrepreneur might also have to influence the market to encourage them to buy the product.

- How big is the market? Who is the competition? How many other companies are offering the same or similar products? Is there room for one more? What market share can your product hope to capture? Is the market trend growing, steady or declining?

- How will the product be better? Will it be more technically efficient and more attractively presented than the competition?

- How much is the market willing to pay for the product? The product must be good value for money, competitive, but also make a profit.

- Where will the customers buy the product? For example, the location of fashion retailers is usually on the High Street.

- When will the customers buy the product? Is there a particular time of the day, week, month, year or season? For example; the end of the month is a high sales period when people are paid, and also the Christmas period when everyone is buying presents.

- Do people know about the product? (advertising and promotions).

- Do people know how to buy the product? (B2B procurement).

- How should the product be packaged and displayed?

- What is the appropriate level of customer support? After sales service and customer support are essential for long term survival and growth.

- How do you get repeat and referred business - consider offering loyalty cards. Repeat business and word of mouth recommendations are not only the most effective form of marketing but, are five times cheaper than creating new business.

The feedback from market research helps the entrepreneur converge on an optimum product or service. All these points come together to form the basis of a coherent marketing plan which is a key component of the business plan. The bottom line is deciding what to sell, to whom, how much and where.

People buy products and services because they feel they need them or want them. It is important to appreciate the difference between **need** and **want**. A person might need a car to drive to work because there is no public transport, compared to wanting a flash BMW to create the right image. Entrepreneurs are particularly good at understanding what the market wants, and tailoring the product to the niche market.

2. Know The Competition

They say '*necessity is the mother of invention*'. Well there is certainly nothing like direct competition to sharpen performance, particularly when coming second does not count, or could greatly reduce the profits.

Keeping an eye on the competitors is an essential component of success, because to be really successful the entrepreneur must offer something better and more attractive than the competitors. A competitor is a business that provides the same or similar products and operates in the same market. The competition can be local, national or, increasingly, international (for example, through the Internet).

There are many ways to develop a competitive edge; the common factor is to achieve a competitive advantage which is recognised by the customers. The product might be technically better than the competitors, but this means nothing if the customers prefer the competitors' features. For example, a family might prefer a basic saloon car compared with a high powered GT with all the 'whistles and bangs'.

There are a number of ways to achieve competitive advantage over the competition. Consider the following:

- **Speed to Market:** The entrepreneur needs to be able to respond quickly to customers needs and new technology - the first to market catches the lion's share.

- **Flexibility:** Small companies, by virtue of their size, should be more flexible than their larger bureaucratic competitors and therefore be able to develop new products quicker. For example, the fashion retailer Zara produces a new clothing range every couple of weeks to respond to the market, whereas large bureaucratic companies such as M&S, traditionally produce clothing ranges for each season.

- **Economy of Scale:** In the long run, as a market grows and stabilises, the large companies usually take over the market because they can afford to invest in R&D and large production runs to achieve economies of scale. This gives them a competitive unit price. For example, in the pioneering days of the car makers and software designers, there were many small companies competing in these growing markets. Over time most of the companies either merged, were taken over, moved to other products, or went bust - leaving a few large multi-national companies in a utility market. As the design stabilizes so the large companies take over and the small entrepreneurial businesses move on to catch the beginning of another technology wave.

- **Personal Service:** A competitive feature of small businesses with a small customer base is that they are able to offer a closer personal service to their

customers - maybe even on a one-to-one basis. Small businesses might also be able to achieve competitive advantage by offering special methods of delivery.

- **Barriers to Entry:** Competitors often impose barriers to entry through copyright, licensing, trade agreements, location (expensive High Street shops) and economy of scale. This of course can also work to the entrepreneur's advantage as they expand.

- **New Products:** Market research suggests that there is a correlation between new products and market performance. New products help to capture and retain market share, leading to increased profitability. For established products it is important to be constantly offering innovative new features to keep the customers interested.

Figure 9.2 outlines a graphical way of comparing your product with your competitor. The ultimate aim should be to become the market leader, as this will not only reduce the competition but also enable you to charge a higher price.

3. Pricing Strategy

The price the entrepreneur decides to charge the customers is mostly a marketing strategy decision. Whilst the entrepreneur needs to determine a base price to cover the expenses, the final price is more the result of where to place the product with respect to the competitors' products and the customers' willingness-to-pay on the supply and demand curve. There are basically three ways to increase profits; cut the costs, increase the sales, or increase the price.

A **penetration price** is a low price to encourage people to buy the product and try it. If they like the product hopefully they will come back for more as repeat customers. In the short term this is an effective marketing strategy for the entrepreneur to build up sales quickly.

Price skimming starts with a high price for a short time period to take advantage of early demand for a new product. This often happens with electronic products, particularly mobile phones and notebook computers. This is a clear willingness-to-pay situation where a small percentage of affluent customers are prepared to pay a higher price to have the latest product now rather than later.

A low price alone might not always be enough to achieve competitive advantage. Unless the entrepreneur's product can achieve a substantial cost advantage over the competitor's product, the entrepreneur should not try to compete on cost alone. Because low prices often bring their own problems as they can only be achieved by cutting the profit margin. Lower profits can lead to a struggle to survive. If you compete aggressively on price, remember the competitors are likely to respond.

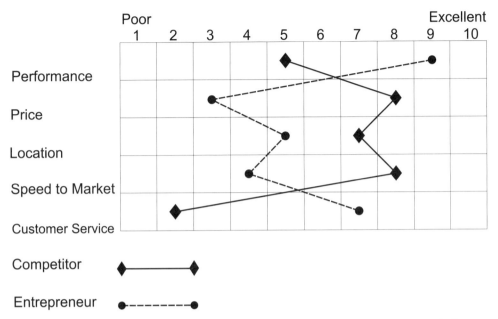

Figure 9.2: Competitor Comparison - By comparing a number of key performance indicators the entrepreneur can quantify their strengths and weaknesses and identify areas to improve

The competitors might even be able to under-cut your price by running at a loss to drive you out of the market, particularly if they have other products to support the loss makers.

4. Location, Location, Location

A company's location is a fundamental part of the marketing plan. For some types of businesses location, location, location is everything. For others it is not as important. For example, a fashion retail shop needs to be in the High Street as part of a cluster of fashion shops, because this is where the majority of shoppers expect to find them, and also where the shop will attract customers from the high volume of passing trade. For other businesses, such as an Internet service provider or office cleaners, the company's location makes no difference to their clients, particularly if the support services travel to their clients' premises.

The location of Richard Branson's first Virgin record shop demonstrated a classic entrepreneurial approach. Branson negotiated free rent to use the room above a shoe shop in Oxford Street. The rationale being that Branson's record shop would bring passing trade to the shoe shop. This symbiotic networking arrangement worked, and established Virgin as a record retailer.

5. Speed to Market

The speed of response to market opportunities is one area where the entrepreneurial company should have competitive advantage over their large company rivals. New technology is continually opening up opportunities - the first new product to market catches the customers.

Small companies, by virtue of their size, should be able to respond quicker to opportunities compared to large companies which have more bureaucratic inertia and an inherent resistance to change. Small companies are also able to make decisions quickly because they are more judgemental and spend less time collecting and analysing data.

Large companies which use a sequential product development process (from one department to another) are being overtaken by companies which use project design teams (where the different departments design their scope of work in parallel). The sequential product development takes much longer than the project team approach where all the departments are represented and the product is designed in parallel.

This situation is reported to have happened at Phillips where, although they were first to the market with their VCR, in the seven years it took them to produce the mark 2 version, a number of Japanese companies had produced three generations and so effectively cornered the market.

The saying goes, *'the big eat the small'*, but now it is, *'**the fast eat the slow**'*. For example, early entry into the market enabled eBay and Amazon to achieve rapid growth and become the market leaders. Getting in first is like a snowball rolling down a hill, gathering more and more customers as it gets bigger. It is a positive spiral - the more sellers the company gets, the more buyers will be looking for a bargain. And by the same argument, the more buyers the company gets, the more sellers will want to offer their products for sale.

However, coming second can also have its advantages - the pioneer is the first to collect the arrows! The first company to market might have to expend a lot of effort establishing a market and sorting out the teething problems. The companies that follow in the second wave can focus on a growing market and developed technology. For example, the search engine market was originally developed by companies such as AltaVista and Ask Jeeves. Google was a late entry, but with the latest technology and a more powerful product they quickly captured the market share and have now capitalised on their success with an IPO.

6. Promoting and Advertising

The final part of the marketing strategy is determining how to tell the potential customers about the product and create an image of the product that stimulates interest. Because a great product which no one knows about will fail - the potential customers will live in ignorance and the entrepreneur will go out of business. It is therefore crucial to get the message across. The promotion strategy should include:

- informing potential customers about the company and the product
- convincing the potential customers your company and your product will satisfy their needs
- enabling the customer to easily find and buy the product
- ensuring that the customer feels the product is affordable but not too cheap (if it is too cheap the customer might be suspicious about its quality!!!).

Who would you give a lift to? Good advertising always helps.

The **company name** or trading name can make or break a business. People associate very closely with company names and product names. Richard Branson for example has put all his effort into making Virgin a brand name which identifies all their products; Virgin Records, Virgin Atlantic, Virgin Blue, Virgin Cola, Virgin Megastore. Stelios Haji-Ioannou has also taken this approach with the easyGroup; easyJet, easyCar, easyCinema and easyInternetcafe.

There is considerable benefit from being able to associate the company name or trading name with the product, where the name immediately conveys a sense of what the product does - Southampton Plumbers, Sydney Electrical, Cape Town Car Hire, LA Bookshop and Vancouver Fashions.

All the methods of communicating contribute to building up the **brand** image. The aim is to achieve instant recognition of the company name or product name and a favourable reaction from the customers. The film *'Bend it Like Beckham'* used the Beckham name to brand the film, which almost certainly contributed to its international success. This works particularly well when the entrepreneur deals directly with the consumer.

Name branding to the end consumer not only protects the product's market share, but can confer valuable protection to the customers against low quality generic no name brands.

Would you pay more for a T-shirt with a designer logo, than a T-shirt without a designer logo? For those that do, the difference in price is clearly the value of the branding.

Advertising: The further the entrepreneur is removed from the customers, the more he needs classic advertising. If the entrepreneur is working through distributors the more he needs to make the public aware of the product and brand.

The reverse is also true – the closer the entrepreneur is to his customers the less he needs to advertise – this is the classic **niche market** position where it is possible to identify the customers directly. For the small business that cannot afford expensive broad based advertising, direct sales might be the most appropriate.

The exception might be when the business is in the early stages of development. At this point branding and image creation will always benefit from broad based advertising.

All business people have to strategise around issues relating to the customers they already have and those they want to attract away from their competitors. It stands to reason that the bigger the company gets, the more formal and complex the marketing strategy will be. But no matter how small or how profitable, the

entrepreneur should not sit back and be satisfied. Change in the business world comes about very quickly. It is important to constantly market the company and the product or service.

For the small business the thought of financing a marketing plan, let alone launching a campaign, can be daunting. Research is expensive, but fortunately a lot of market research relies on gut feelings. The entrepreneur's marketing plan, campaign and evaluation are all geared towards accomplishing two basic goals:

- value to the consumer
- profit to the entrepreneur.

Exercises:

1. Discuss how you have linked your product's features to the market's needs.
2. Outline how you would conduct your market research.
3. Using figure 9.2 develop a marketing comparison between your product and your competitor's product.

Instructor's Manual: An Instructor's Manual is available with additional exercises and case studies, see *<www.knowledgezone.net>*.

10
Networking

LEARNING OUTCOMES - enables the reader to:

Appreciate the concept - it is not what you know, it is who you know that opens the doors of opportunity.

Evaluate the stakeholder analysis.

Understand the benefits of technology clusters, science parks and incubators.

Discuss the benefits of having a mentor to guide the entrepreneur through the start up phase of a new venture.

They say "*It's not what you know – it's who you know*" that opens the doors of opportunity. In the entrepreneur's case it is the ability to network with a broad range of contacts who give advice, information and resources to make the entrepreneur's product or service.

Networking skills are possibly the **most important** entrepreneurial trait helping the entrepreneur achieve success. The entrepreneur's ability to develop a network of helpful contacts far outweighs any portfolio of academic degrees and certificates of employment (the '*old-school-tie*' **who** you know has always been acknowledged as being more important than **what** you know). Although what you know usually influences who you know in the first place!

Through a network of contacts the entrepreneur uses the back door to beg, borrow and befriend, to gain access to ideas, information and resources to make the product. This could be ideas to solve a design problem, the free use of equipment to solve a manufacturing problem, or the late payment of an invoice to help the cashflow.

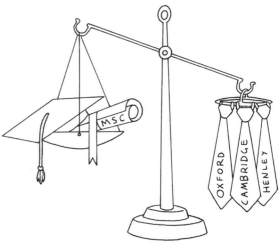

".... contacts out weigh degrees...."

"Hi, may I use your computer for a research project?"

For example, during Bill Gates' humble beginnings he is reported to have written his first commercial programme (BASIC) discretely using Harvard University's mainframe computer, together with help from fellow students (computers were big, rare and expensive in those days). This is a classic entrepreneurial networking approach to getting started – to gain free access to useful facilities and also free contributions from willing helpers. This way entrepreneurs keep their costs as low as possible, which reduces the financial risk.

1. Stakeholder Analysis

Entrepreneurs do not operate in a vacuum; they work within a company, within an industry and within a market. Networking is the entrepreneur's lifeblood - it is really too important a commodity to leave to chance. All successful entrepreneurs will almost certainly have developed their network of contacts in a proactive manner. This section will show how an entrepreneur can use a stakeholder analysis to identify the key stakeholders. A stakeholder might be defined as any organisation or person (both internal and external):

- who is actively involved in the venture or business
- whose interests are affected by the venture being implemented
- who could have an affect on the venture, for example, the Green lobby.

It is obviously in the entrepreneur's interests to identify all the stakeholders to determine their needs and expectations so they can be integrated with the venture's objectives. The entrepreneur should create an environment where the stakeholders are encouraged to contribute their skills and knowledge as this might be useful to the success of the venture. These needs and expectations should then be managed, influenced and balanced to ensure a successful outcome. Consider the following headings:

- **Originator:** The originator is the entrepreneur who suggested the innovative idea or spotted the opportunity in the first place.
- **Owner:** The owner is the person, department or company whose strategic plan created the need for the venture.
- **Sponsor:** The sponsor is the company or client who will authorise expenditure for the venture - this could be an internal client.
- **Retailers:** Outlets that sell the products.
- **Users:** The people who will use or operate the product on behalf of the owner.
- **Customers:** The people who receive and pay for the benefit of using the product or service (for example, electricity or mobile phones).
- **Boss:** The person you report to can play an important role in establishing your working environment, the support you receive and your career prospects within the organisation.

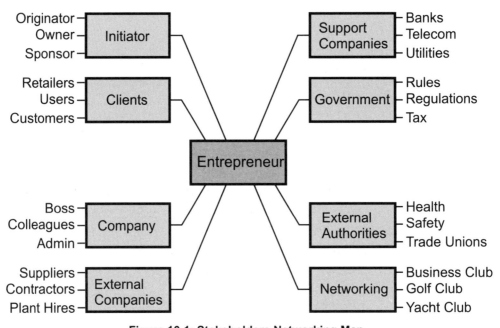

Figure 10.1: Stakeholders Networking Map

- **Colleagues:** Although your work colleagues or team members might not be working on the same venture, indirectly they can supply useful background information and peer support.
- **Admin:** The company's administration keeps the wheels of information turning.
- **Suppliers:** The suppliers of materials and consumables have a wealth of specialised experience about their product.
- **Contractors:** The contractors or people who design and build the facility for the owner.
- **Plant Hire:** The suppliers of plant hire and lease equipment.
- **Finance:** Banks, venture capital and any other source of finance.
- **Support Companies:** Suppliers of services; telecoms, electricity, water.
- **Government:** Rules and regulations, Health & Safety, and taxes.
- **External:** Quality standards, and Trade Unions.
- **Networking Organisations:** Chamber of Commerce, Business Clubs, Golf Clubs, and Yacht Clubs.

It is the entrepreneur's responsibility to build coalitions among the various stakeholders in the venture. This is a proactive way of gaining power and influence.

The stakeholders can be further subdivided into the stakeholders who are only interested in the venture while it is being implemented, and the stakeholders who are only interested in the outcome of the venture. The first group could be people working on the venture (say fitting out a restaurant), and the second group could be people who use the venture (say customers of a restaurant).

Stakeholders can be further classified into those who are positively affected by the venture and those that are negatively affected by the venture. In this situation the positively affected could compensate the negatively affected parties. Consider a dam project – the people whose land is flooded could be compensated by the people who use the water and electricity supplied by the dam.

The stakeholders can also be subdivided into those that support the venture, and those that oppose it. It is important to equally address those who oppose the venture and discuss their fears, because it is these stakeholders that could derail the venture. Some of their concerns might be valid and, with some flexibility, could be accommodated. At the end of the day the entrepreneur might not be able to please all the stakeholders and, in this conflict environment, the entrepreneur will need to establish a priority of stakeholders' needs and make decisions accordingly.

2. Symbiotic Continuum

Networking for information and resources to solve problems and improve the company's competitive advantage implies a one way flow of benefit. But entrepreneurs are generally very good at looking after their contacts - where possible they reciprocate useful information and do not bleed them dry!!! Rather than feeling exploited, entrepreneurs' contacts often end up as life long friends and continue to help the entrepreneur in their ventures over the years. Consider this wildlife analogy of a continuum of possible relationships an entrepreneur can have with his contacts;

- Host
- Parasite
- Symbiotic
- Paternal (breast feeding)

Host: The host analogy bleeds their victim dry while they grow fat on the host and eventually kill it. This was graphically shown in the film '*Aliens*'. In the entrepreneurial context this would be taking from the host until the host's company was eventually put out of business. The Al Capone approach comes to mind.

Parasite: The parasite analogy is more realistic where the parasite lives off the prey but does not kill it. In the entrepreneurial context this would relate to continually taking small amounts of information and 'borrowing' resources from the contact, but giving nothing back. They parasite is more of a nuisance than anything else.

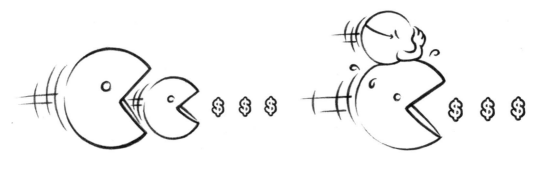

Host   Parasite

Symbiotic: The symbiotic analogy is the classic entrepreneur networking type of relationship. Here each party lives together for mutual benefit. A marine example is the symbiotic relationship between the tropical coral reefs and the algae that lives inside the coral polyps. The algae processes the sunlight which gives the coral its beautiful array of colours, and the coral gives the algae a home. In the entrepreneurial context this would be the entrepreneur taking information and resources from his contact, but at the same time giving back useful information and resources, making it a two way sharing and collaborative exchange.

Paternal: The paternal analogy relates to giving and not expecting anything back in return. This would be like the mother breast feeding her child. For the mother it is return enough to see her child grow up strong and healthy. In the entrepreneurial context this would be the **mentor** freely giving the entrepreneur advice to give them direction and solve their problems - and not expect any payment in return. Like the mother, the business mentor is pleased to give their advice. The mentor's reward is seeing the entrepreneur prosper and grow. Perhaps there is a sense of giving back to society as a return for the help he received as a young person.

The symbiotic relationship is obviously the type of relationship to aim for, where '*I scratch your back and you scratch my back*', because this relationship is a win-win situation which will benefit both parties and ultimately stand the test of time. This situation also relates to favours - '*one good turn deserves another*'. If you want to call in a favour, you have a better chance of getting what you want if you have been generous with your time and contacts in the first place – it is a two way street.

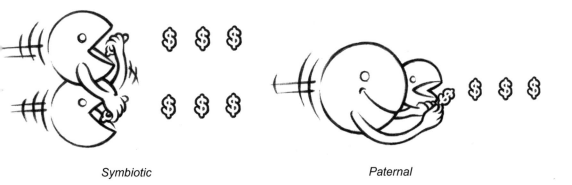

Symbiotic   Paternal

3. Technology Clusters

When a number of companies using similar technology set up in the same area this is called a technology cluster. The Silicon Valley cluster in California is well known for developing the personal computer.

Technology clusters are not a new phenomenon. Two hundred years ago traders and merchants would meet in the coffee houses in London and other trading centres to hear the latest news on commodity prices, keep up with political gossip and make business deals. The great insurance company, Lloyds of London, actually developed from Lloyds Coffee House in Fenchurch St in 1771. Lloyds Coffee House was a meeting place for captains, shipowners and merchants who wanted to hear the latest maritime news.

Silicon Valley: Silicon Valley comprises of a cluster of entrepreneurial companies which have all come together to collectively form an entrepreneurial computer industry where the region as a whole performs like one large entrepreneurial company. The Silicon Valley cluster has all the key ingredients and critical mass to work effectively as a technology cluster:

- universities (supplying wiz kids)
- entrepreneurs networking in the local bars and clubs (creating a cross-flow of ideas)
- research parks (developing the latest technology)
- venture capital companies (funding new ventures)
- local hightech industry (manufacturing and producing the latest technology)
- spin-off companies (developing new technology which keeps the cluster at the leading edge).

Stanford University and other Californian universities are a continuous source of academic wiz kids. Stanford University's Research Park, set up by Professor Fred Terman, supports research and development but, most importantly, encourages the entrepreneurial spirit in the students. The development of the Research Park also gives the cluster credibility which encourages venture capitalists and large corporations like Lockheed Aerospace, IBM and Xerox to move into the area and give the cluster critical mass.

In Silicon Valley people are openly encouraged to network informally in groups like the Home Brew Computer Club, and meet in the bars and cafes such as the Mountain View restaurant, or the Walker's Wagon Wheel bar. In this social environment, the computer engineers freely talk about the latest technology being

developed, the problems and opportunities. This atmosphere of cross-fertilizing ideas and gossip is an effective way of transferring technology and disseminating information. And when they see their peers developing creative ideas into leading edge products and successful companies - this further encourages and inspires the entrepreneurial spirit.

The technology cluster approach is successful for Silcon Valley because the work practices have changed from being secretive and confrontational to a culture of openness, working together, breaking down barriers and co-operation. **Collaboration** is a powerful word in Silicon Valley. The technology cluster encourages the development of strategic alliances with other companies in the computer industry. This enables each company to focus on what they do best, enabling them to produce products quicker, reduce unit cost and ultimately grow faster.

Spin-off companies occur when someone leaves an established company to set up a new company to develop their new creative ideas. Computer companies mature fast in Silicon Valley, so part of the cluster's competitiveness is the spin-off companies that continually keep Silicon Valley at the leading edge.

Two famous spin-off companies are HP and Google, and they in turn have spawned other spin-off companies. Bill Hewlett and Dave Packard's spin-off company developed out of Stanford University's Research Park and was initially set up in a garage in 1938. Larry Page and Sergey Brin of Google had worked for other Internet search engine companies (which included Alta Vista) before starting their own spin-off search engine company.

4. Science Parks

The concept of science parks operating close to universities has caught on around the world. They come under a variety of local names; silicon glens, silicon fens, and technology parks. They all offer similar benefits to entrepreneurs; cheap office space, cheap business infrastructure, and tax breaks. The aim is to boost the creativity and the productivity of all the companies within the cluster by fostering opportunities for collaboration and the exchange of information.

Incubators are part of the science park concept, except they are formally sponsored by public and private investors to help small businesses and entrepreneurs overcome many of the problems they could encounter during the start up phase. The incubator can provide hands-on management assistance, shared office services, access to equipment, a resource pool, flexible leases, and access to finance - all under one roof.

The incubator approach can reduce overhead costs by sharing facilities, sharing computer systems (hardware and software), sharing admin, combining bulk purchases and shipping (giving an economy of scale), and might even share marketing promotions.

In the incubator the budding entrepreneur will be able to speak to other entrepreneurs who have already gone through the process of setting up their own businesses and should have the start up experiences still fresh in their minds. This is an excellent environment for the new entrepreneur to test out their creative ideas and get immediate feedback. The incubator is like one-stop networking all under one roof, together with formal government sponsored handholding to get the entrepreneur started.

The time spent in the incubator is usually limited - typically two years. The objective is to get the fledgling business off the ground, up and running profitably, so the entrepreneur can leave the nest and prosper.

5. Famous Clusters

Most industries benefit from being part of a technology cluster. All of us are probably operating within a cluster of some description. Consider the following:

Oil Cluster: London and Houston are the two main technology clusters for the oil industry - this is where the oil giants have their head offices. If you want to do business in the oil industry these are the two cities to start looking for contacts.

Film Cluster: Although there are many national film industries producing blockbuster movies - the big two are Hollywood and Bollywood. Hollywood is THE place for actors, producers, directors, writers and agents to network - to see and be seen. Hollywood is also the place where film makers arrange finance and distribution contracts.

Fashion Cluster: The fashion industry has small clusters centred around most cities - but the big three are London, Paris and New York. These clusters include all the support industries which enable them to achieve competitive advantage. This would include the fashion designers who design the clothing, fashion marketing agencies, fashion shows, fashion magazines, fashion retail shops, and even the fashion schools to teach the trade (most of the clothing manufacture was outsourced to the East long ago).

Sports Cluster: National sport teams benefit from the sport cluster that underpins the national side. Whether the sport is rugby, football or netball, they all need a continuous supply of young talent moving up the hierarchy; from the schools, to local teams, to county teams, and eventually to represent the national team. The cluster in a wider sense also includes the stadiums, supporters, media, press, sports trainers, sports coaches, sports doctors, sports clothing and sports equipment manufacturers.

6. Mentors

Mentors are usually experienced business people (often previously entrepreneurs themselves) who have a wealth of experience in the business environment and offer their advice to start up entrepreneurs to help guide them through the pitfalls and minefields that can occur.

Poor business management practices have derailed many start up companies. This is compounded by entrepreneurs who are reluctant to ask for help - until it is too late. To overcome this problem small businesses are encouraged to network with mentors who have a wealth of technical and business experience. Lending institutions often link their loans to the entrepreneur gaining mentor support. They want to see that there is a safe pair of hands guiding the business through the start up phase.

"....hello, I'm looking for a mentor...."

For budding entrepreneurs who are bursting with innovative ideas and who want to get going as quickly as possible, developing basic business requirements are more than likely going to be overlooked. This is where the mentor can help the entrepreneur focus on the key issues:

- quantify creative ideas and the product's strengths and weaknesses
- access market research to confirm there is a demand for the product
- sources of finance and government grants
- access to resources and equipment
- help develop the business plan
- ensure all the management systems are in place - this might include: budgets, admin, production, credit control, cash flow, information systems, marketing and human resources
- information on tax issues
- information on health and safety, and employment law
- growth potential and growth strategy.

As a one-on-one coach, the mentor's mission is to take on promising, but unseasoned, first-time entrepreneurs and help them develop their ideas into a viable business.

Mentors usually offer their advice free to the small business entrepreneur. This is their way of putting something back into society. Their reward is in seeing the business get started, seeing it survive the initial phases and grow into a prosperous company. But beware, free advice from a poor man might turn out to be expensive!!!

Mentors are typically no longer interested in starting their own company, but still love the thrill of the start up business. They love the creative process of being part of an innovative team, but they do not want the 24/7 lifestyle, working all hours of the day and night. Mentors are motivated by their desire to share their hard-won experience, and to see their protégés succeed.

The hard work is up to the entrepreneur and their team. Having a mentor can be a huge support and can help the entrepreneur see the wood from the trees. First time entrepreneurs often fail because they do not have a more experienced mentor from whom they can learn and turn to for advice - everyone needs a sounding board.

7. Internet

The Internet has become a very efficient platform for the entrepreneur to network and make contacts. Where entrepreneurs used to meet in coffee shops, trade exchanges and business clubs, they can now meet on the Internet where vast amounts of information are available through search engines and chat rooms - all at the click of a mouse. The enormous growth of the Internet has fuelled the demand for chatrooms and in turn has created opportunities for networking. Consider the following:

- the Internet makes round-the-clock sharing of information possible - this was one of the motivators for Tim Berners-Lee developing the Internet in the first place
- the Internet enables global networking across the time zones
- the Internet encourages the emergence of horizontal communities bound together by a common interest - these communities can easily float ideas between each other
- the value of the Internet lies in its capacity to store, analyse, and communicate information instantly, anywhere at negligible cost.

Cultivating business and social contacts is like nurturing a tree to grow - done successfully, the branches will grow into other branches, so that, ultimately, the entrepreneur will have access to someone who knows, or someone who knows someone who knows.

Having gone to the enormous effort of establishing a comprehensive network of contacts the next step is to maintain them. As the list gets bigger, the entrepreneur needs to formalise the network list on to a data base, so it can be developed into a contact plan. The frequency obviously depends on the type of business, but once or twice a year should be a minimum - it does not go down well to only contact someone when you need something!!!

Exercises:

1. Identify your key stakeholders and subdivide them into a number of distinct categories.

2. Discuss a symbiotic business relationship you have where there is a two way transfer of ideas and information.

3. Identify the technology cluster you work in, and discuss how it influences and benefits your business.

Instructor's Manual: An Instructor's Manual is available with additional exercises and case studies, see *<www.knowledgezone.net>*.

11
Negotiation

LEARNING OUTCOMES - enables the reader to:
Understand the difference between the three negotiation strategies; win-lose strategy; win-win strategy; and the lose-lose strategy.
Develop a negotiation tactic plan of action.
Know how to negotiate.
Understand the dispute process.

Negotiation is the art of influencing people to make them see things your way!!! The other party will of course be trying to influence you to see things their way. And so we have a dynamic situation of opposing positions which can only be amicably resolved by negotiation.

Negotiation is the process of trying to get a better deal than you would get without negotiation. If you do not ask for a discount when shopping, for example, then you will not get it!

Negotiation differs from direct control, where people can exercise their authority to obtain compliance. An entrepreneur would not normally have direct authority over all their stakeholders; maybe some vendors, but certainly not their clients. So, to be successful an entrepreneur must develop and use negotiation techniques to achieve the best deals with their clients and suppliers.

Networking and negotiation skills come naturally for many entrepreneurs. This may well be why they have taken the entrepreneurial route in the first place but, as with most management techniques, there is an underlying structure which influences and constrains how to operate. This chapter sets out some of these negotiating techniques. The three basic negotiation strategies are:

- win-lose strategy (you win they lose)
- win-win strategy (you both win)
- lose-lose strategy (you both lose).

1. Win-Lose Strategy

If the entrepreneur adopts a win-lose strategy this means he is trying to win a negotiation (winner takes all) against an opponent who must lose or, at best, not achieve their targets.

The win-lose strategy is a competitive adversarial bargaining approach where each party is searching for the other party's weaknesses and will then capitalise on any weaknesses discovered. Until quite recently this was the normal way to do business in many industries.

The consequence of this approach is there is little or no sharing of information with the other party and consequently no attempt is made to understand the other party's needs and expectations. There is also very **little trust** between the parties, which essentially kills effective two way communication and goodwill. Everyone is playing their cards very close to their chest, being careful not to give anything away.

The win-lose strategy forces one party to give in and modify their position by compromise and concession. This negotiation strategy may be effective, when there is a 'fixed size' pie to be divided. So the smaller your opponents share, the bigger your share. It may also be considered a viable scenario when the underlying aim is to eliminate potential competitors.

2. Win-Win Strategy

The win-win strategy is a **collaborative** approach where each party is trying to achieve the best deal for both parties - a mutually agreeable solution.

Information is openly shared between parties in order to improve their understanding of each other's position (needs and expectations). Efforts are made to learn about all the problems and constraints facing each party - now and in the future.

For the win-win strategy to succeed, there has to be a demonstrable climate of trust and honesty between the parties that allows an open exchange of views and expectations. Both parties must be genuinely interested in solving their differences. Each party is therefore looking for strengths to build on, not weaknesses to use to defeat the other party. Usually this level of mutual trust will only come about where both parties are striving to develop long term commercial relationships.

Each party has to appreciate that they are probably not going to achieve their ideal solution, but they want to work with the other party to find the middle ground and settlement range which is acceptable to both parties (see figure 11.1).

Through collaborative discussion and joint problem-solving, the parties might actually discover a third way - an innovative option which has not yet been considered. This option could be an even better alternative than each party's original position. This would definitely be a win-win solution.

The success of the computer industry cluster in Silicon Valley can be partly attributed to collaboration between the various computer designers and engineers. There are plenty of bars and clubs to meet socially and network. This informal exchange of information, symbiotic relationships and problem-solving keeps the industry as a whole at the forefront of technology. This is a classic win-win environment.

The win-win strategy is essential when the other party's input and commitment are crucial to achieving the desired outcomes now and in the future.

3. Lose-Lose Strategy

If you adopt the lose-lose strategy you are basically saying "*If I lose* [the contract] *I am going to make sure you lose* [the contract] *as well*". Unless there are good business reasons to adopt this spiteful strategy, you may be making unnecessary enemies which could come back to haunt you in later negotiations. It is far better for long term business relationships to ensure each party leaves the negotiation table having won something (the win-win situation).

4. Negotiation Tactics

The following negotiation tactics outline a number of useful approaches which should improve the chances of getting a better deal.

Prepare: Do your homework and find out what are the needs and expectations of the other parties. This is essential no matter what negotiating strategy you intend using. You may have to do this informally through a network of contacts. Knowing how keen the other party is to buy or sell may influence their **settlement range**. (See section on Bargaining, to establish your opponents' settlement range).

Battle Plan: Before negotiating it is sensible to establish a battle plan outlining what you want to achieve, and how you plan to achieve it (together with options). It is also important to establish your bottom line (particularly at an auction) to decide at which point you walk away from the deal.

Exaggerate: Start by exaggerating your position or requirement in order to weaken the other party's argument and so lower their resistance to your real objectives. Similarly, regard the comments by your opponents as over statements of their position and so try to devalue them. It is a fact that those with high aspirations in life often achieve better results. In negotiation, high demands and hard-fought concessions often lower the other side's aspiration level.

Frequent Meetings: Try to organise frequent meetings between parties to enable tentative ideas to be quietly eased into the discussion. The continual probing and sounding out of possibilities enables embryonic ideas to establish and grow. Whereas, new ideas formally presented without notice at the monthly meeting are quite likely to be rejected.

Temporary Opinions: Unlike attitudes, opinions are often temporary and could change over time. If a party rejects your initial offer out of hand on Monday, by Friday, after thinking about it all week, they might well have softened their views and have moved closer to your position. Therefore it could be self-defeating to push the other party into a corner straight away, as this might make them cast their opinions in stone. If possible always leave the door open so that you can revisit a proposal.

Solve Easy Differences First: Try to solve the easy differences first to show progress, good faith and willingness on your side to compromise and search for middle ground. This helps to set a collaborative tone for the following negotiations as you move on to the more difficult issues.

Give Concessions On Minor Issues: Give concessions on minor issues, especially if they are not important to you, but are important to the other party. This might encourage the other party to similarly make concessions on their position, which are important to you.

Force The Issue: Forcing the issue by setting ultimatums and deadlines might trick the other party into revealing their bottom line and settlement range.

Social Pressures: Social pressures can influence how a person negotiates. For example, a subordinate might appear as a '*yes man*' when negotiating with their superior. An awareness of possible cultural pressures is more important when negotiating with companies from other countries who might well put a high level of importance on cultural and racial correctness.

5. Bargaining

Bargaining is the process of giving up something to gain something - preferably giving up a little to gain a lot. To bargain effectively you need to exaggerate your position and understate or diminish the other party's position - this gives you room to *'negotiate'*.

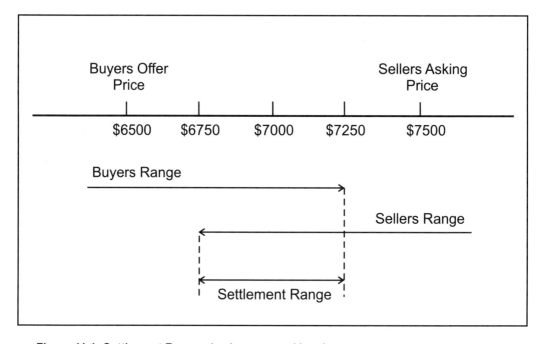

Figure 11.1: Settlement Range - buying a second hand car

It is a natural human trait to barter and trade. For example, when buying a second hand car we usually 'negotiate' over the price. The buyer and seller know this, so the seller will usually ask for slightly more than they expect, and the buyer usually offers slightly less than they are prepared to pay. For example, if the asking price for the car is $7500 – then the buyer offers $6500 and, after some horse-trading, both parties will probably agree on $7000.

The settlement range is the area of mutually agreeable solutions. In the settlement range both parties would rather compromise from their initial position, than stop the deal. There are times, however, when negotiation would be very tedious. For example, imagine trying to negotiate at the checkout for every item in your supermarket trolley.

6. Networking Skills

Networking skills are an important part of negotiation because they enable the entrepreneur to gain a better deal from someone they '*know*'. People are far more likely to help someone they like and trust than someone they do not know - someone who cold calls off the street as it were. The *Networking* chapter discusses how to identify the key stakeholders who can help the entrepreneur achieve competitive advantage.

7. Dispute Resolution

If the differences with another party cannot be resolved by negotiation, there are a number of dispute resolution processes to consider; arbitration, mediation and conciliation.

Arbitration: Arbitration is a legal alternative to litigation where the parties in dispute agree to submit their respective positions to a neutral third party for resolution.

Mediation: Mediation is a dispute resolution process where a neutral third party, the mediator or facilitator, assists the parties in order to help them achieve an agreement.

Conciliation: Conciliation is similar to mediation, except the conciliator meets with the parties separately in an attempt to resolve their differences.

A method of dispute resolution should be included in all contract agreements at the outset because, once a dispute situation arises, the parties may not be able to agree on anything, never mind a dispute resolution process.

Exercises:

1. Give examples where you have used the three negotiating strategies; win-lose, win-win, and lose-lose.

2. Discuss how you have used collaboration to negotiate a better deal.

3. Discuss what negotiation tactics you would use to buy a house or car.

Instructor's Manual: An Instructor's Manual is available with additional exercises and case studies, see <*www.knowledgezone.net*>.

12
Sources of Finance

Ready cash and seed money are the life-blood of entrepreneur start up ventures. Without sufficient funds the new venture's success will be self-limited, because there simply will not be funds and resources available to develop, manufacture and market the product.

Calculating how much money an entrepreneur needs to get started and how much money the entrepreneur can raise are probably two sides of the same coin – as one influences the other. As a starting point the entrepreneur probably has a rough estimate of both but, at some point, the entrepreneur should formalise his thinking with a coherent business plan. The financial requirements can be subdivided into four main funding areas;

- development capital
- start up capital
- stocking capital
- working capital (cash flow).

Development capital is required to develop the product. This might involve a feasibility study which includes product design, model testing, building a prototype, and market research to confirm there is a market for the product.

Start up capital is required to establish the product or service. This may involve buying or renting premises, buying or leasing equipment, buying material and hiring labour. Other start up costs could include office admin, and distribution, together with marketing and advertising to promote the product.

Stocking capital is required to build up stock of the product or service. There is a trade-off here between long production runs to lower the unit cost, but with higher warehouse costs; compared with short production runs with a higher unit cost, but with lower warehouse costs. Once the stock has been built up the converse is also true - destocking gives an amazing boost to the cash flow.

Working capital is required to even out any short term dips in the monthly cash flow between income and expenditure.

Product development capital, start up capital and stocking capital are essentially all up front costs, while working capital is required to iron out any short term cash flow fluctuations.

1. Networking

Through their network of contacts entrepreneurs might be able to beg or borrow the resources they need to start their ventures. This is a classic entrepreneurial approach to obtain the free use of resources to gain competitive advantage. This would obviously be one of the first sources of assistance to consider (see *Networking* chapter).

2. Personal Funds

Personal funds are the most common source of start up funding. Entrepreneurs are always going to have to dip into their own pockets first, even if it is only to show potential investors they are totally committed.

The advantage of using personal finance is that it is the least expensive source of finance to obtain, and it gives the entrepreneur the greatest level of control (or the least amount of outside interference), and the maximum level of profit. But the disadvantage is, it also means the entrepreneur carries all the risk.

Banks and venture capital firms investing in a new venture will want to see that the entrepreneur is financially committed to the enterprise. So that if the going gets tough, the entrepreneur will be highly motivated to work through the problems and not throw in the towel at the first obstacle.

A second mortgage on the entrepreneur's house to release funds, should not be considered as a personal loan from a bank for the venture. Because a mortgage is a loan to buy a house and not a loan from the bank to set up a new venture, although the funds might be used for that purpose.

 cosmic mba series

3. Family and Friends

After networking and personal finance, family and friends are the third and fourth most common source of finance for new ventures. This is clearly because they want to support the entrepreneur (this could go both ways of course).

Acquiring start up capital from family and friends sounds a bit amateurish from a business management point of view, but research clearly indicates that few start up companies are able to source venture capital from banks and other institutions during their start up phase (see figure 12.3: Life Cycle Finance).

A loan from family and friends means they are backing the entrepreneur personally and therefore might not need convincing with a business plan and cash flow statement. This means they can be approached in the early stages of the start up phase.

A loan from family and friends would probably be unstructured and therefore might be perceived to be an equity stake where they would not only expect their capital returned and a return on their investment, but also a share in the new venture's profit.

Family and friends are generally understanding investors who are likely to be more patient than institutional investors in wanting their money back by a certain date. But in this uncertain relationship, although family and friends might be perceived as equity investors, if the enterprise fails, they would probably expect the loan to be paid back in full.

4. Credit Card

Credit card finance is one of the easiest to obtain and is a very practical way of providing short term funds to cover the payment for goods and materials – the entrepreneur might even get some user points!!! Credit cards offer between 30 to 60 days of free credit before a payment is required. Credit card interest rates are very expensive, so they should not be used as a long term source of finance.

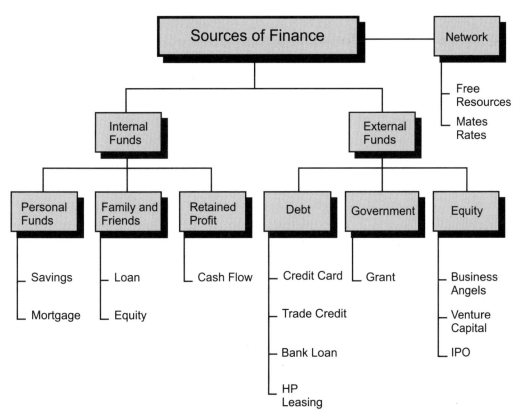

Figure 12.1: Sources of Finance (as a breakdown structure)

5. Trade Credit

Trade credit is really a cash flow loan where a supplier gives the entrepreneur credit for 30, 60 or 90 days before they require payment for their goods and services. This is essentially an interest free short-term loan. Trade credit is the most easily accessible external source of short-term finance for entrepreneurs and the simplest to negotiate. Consider:

- If no cash discount is offered for early payment and the payment is due 30 days after delivery, then only pay on the 30th day.
- Whenever possible negotiate with the supplier for a payment extension. For example, if the terms are 30 days from receipt, try and extend it to 30 days from the end of the month. This could extend the payment by a couple of weeks.

Trade credit has been the make or break opportunity many entrepreneurs have used to get started, where they obtain the materials to perform a job and receive payment from their client before paying their suppliers. This is living life on the edge, but if it gets the entrepreneur started and money in the bank, then this is a route to consider.

Giving extended credit to clients, distributors and retailers impacts negatively on the entrepreneur's cash flow - this is trade credit in reverse. In this situation the entrepreneur is paying for the manufacture and supply of the product before they receive payment from their client. This is obviously not to be encouraged. Giving extended credit and consignment stock can lead to a vicious circle of chasing debts and fending off suppliers because the entrepreneur cannot afford to pay them.

6. Retained Profit

Retained profits are an obvious source of finance as the product and company become established. This is the preferred route of finance for lifestyle companies as they plough back the profits to achieve sustainable growth.

7. Banks

The commercial high street banks are a logical source of short and long term finance for entrepreneurial ventures. The availability of these loans can be influenced by the entrepreneur's relationship with the bank. The bank manager could be a key stakeholder in the venture, so should be part of the entrepreneur's network of contacts. Banks are risk adverse institutions, so they like to see that the entrepreneur has done his homework in the format they prefer – a business plan. A business plan enables the bank manager to assess the risk of the proposal (see section on Business Plans).

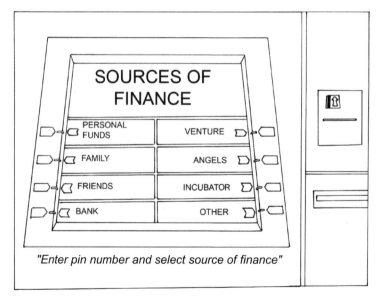

"Enter pin number and select source of finance"

The business plan should clearly present the strength of the venture, supported with realistic cash flow projections. The banks place a higher emphasis on the cash flow projections than the entrepreneur might realise. Although bank loans might be secured by a disposable asset (for example a house), in practice the repayments can only come from positive cash flow – which is why the cash flow projections are so important. Other considerations are:

- the entrepreneur's previous work experience and demonstrable skills in the field of the venture
- credit rating and financial track record
- personal investment in the venture.

Banks like to see that the entrepreneur is totally committed to make the investment work, so the banks are more likely to support the entrepreneur dollar for dollar, a gearing of 1:1.

Banks are becoming more interested in the personality of the people they lend funds to, because they want to try to determine how the entrepreneur is going to respond to problems and set backs? As more MBA graduates become bank managers so they are asking borrowers take **psychometric tests**. Psychometric testing is finding favour in the city because there is a surge of management buyouts where the strength of key individuals is key to the success of the enterprise.

Short term finance in the form of an **overdraft** is nearly always used as working capital to cover negative cash flow. This could happen at any time during the business cycle, therefore, most companies would normally have an overdraft facility in place.

The banks also have their own cash flow constraints, so it is important that the entrepreneur keeps the bank informed if he is getting close to the overdraft limit. The entrepreneur must never knowingly go over the overdraft limit without discussing it with the bank first, otherwise future overdraft facilities will be more difficult to obtain.

Fast growing businesses must anticipate negative cash flows as they battle to control uncertain cash flow projections. It is a fact that more companies go into liquidation due to negative cash flow than for any other reason.

Leasing and hire purchase are popular methods to finance cars and capital equipment because the repayments are spread over a few years. The lease company buys the equipment the entrepreneur wants and leases it back in return for regular lease payments (usually monthly). These payments are tax deductible when the equipment is used to produce an income. Delaying payment for capital equipment will have a positive short-term effect on the cash flow which will give the entrepreneur some breathing space to get the venture established.

8. Business Angels

Business angels are usually wealthy private investors who are willing to provide small amounts of their own capital to seed entrepreneurial ventures, unlike the institutional venture capital companies, who invest other people's money. Business angels not only bring an injection of funds into the venture, but also a wealth of entrepreneurial experience and contacts which can be invaluable for a fledgling start up.

The business angels naturally want to make a return on their investment, but they also want to share in the excitement of seeing an idea become a reality, and are more relaxed about the time it takes for the venture to come to fruition. Business angel investing is on the increase as a growing number of individuals seek better returns on their money than they can get from traditional investments.

Business angels, typically, are wealthy individuals who have made their own pile of cash through their own entrepreneurial endeavours, so they understand the entrepreneurial process. They will be able to help the entrepreneur develop a business plan and know how to apply for government grants.

Typically, these investors bring a lot more than just cash to the venture and will, through a place on the board, offer advice and experience to help develop the business over time. In many cases, small early stage companies require less equity than many venture capital companies want to invest, whereas the business angels are able to fill this funding void and invest smaller amounts.

A word of warning about business angels - remember they were probably entrepreneurs in their own right and by definition are strong-willed, single-minded individuals who might have an agenda of their own. Unless both parties agree on the business strategy this route might be creating problems further down the line.

9. Venture Capital

Venture capital companies professionally manage a pool of equity capital. The equity pool is usually formed from the resources of wealthy partners, pension funds, endowment funds, large corporations and other institutions. The pool is managed by a venture capital firm in exchange for a percentage of the investment.

As a result, the venture capital companies tend to have deeper pockets than other investors but they also have obligations to their investors and are, therefore, more circumspect about which companies they invest in.

The purpose of venture capital firms is to generate long-term capital appreciation through debt and equity investments. Venture capital firms are therefore looking for entrepreneurial companies with good growth prospects.

The venture capital firm will probably want a seat on the board so that they can support the management team, to ensure their investment can prosper.

Venture capital firms in the UK typically invest between £100,000 to £10 million in growth companies. But if you think raising funds from a venture capital firm is going to be easy think again. Many of the major venture capital firms will receive literally thousands of business plans, listen to pitches from hundreds of start up companies, and ultimately fund less than one per cent. In other words, the odds do not favour the average entrepreneur.

Venture capital firms are looking for a high return on their investment in the form of capital gain rather than dividends. Their **exit strategy** is usually by selling an equity stake to another company, or an IPO flotation on a stock market.

Incubators: (see *Networking* chapter) Incubators and science parks are established to help small business entrepreneurs overcome many of the problems they might encounter during the start up phase. Incubators are usually found in business parks where part of the package includes introductions to government grants, business angels and venture capital firms.

10. Debit or Equity Financing

There are two basic ways of acquiring finance;

- Debt – borrowings, which involve repayment
- Equity – share capital, which gives ownership

Selecting the type of finance or the balance between the two is a risk management assessment. Debt finance will increase the entrepreneur's share of the profits, but increase his exposure to risk. While equity finance will reduce the entrepreneur's exposure to risk, but also reduce his share of the profits.

Debit finance (borrowing funds from a bank) requires the loan to be paid in full plus interest, irrespective of the sales and profits. The bank typically requires collateral (a house or land) to reduce their risk exposure. Although the borrower appears to be carrying all the risk, the advantage is that when the new venture does really well, the borrower will keep all the profits. However, if the company goes belly-up all the money loaned from the bank will still have to be repaid in full.

Equity finance is where an outside investor takes some form of equity or ownership (share holding) in the new venture. They do not require collateral or interest payments from the entrepreneur, but they do want to share the profit of the enterprise on a pro rata basis (and will accept a share of the loss). This has the advantage of limiting the risk, but the disadvantage for the entrepreneur of having to share the profits (and maybe control). However, if the company goes belly-up the entrepreneur simply loses his investment but, walks away to fight another day without any debts to pay off.

	Cost to Borrow	Level of Control	Profits	Risk
Networking	Low	High	High	Low
Personal Funds	Low	High	High	High
Family and Friends	Medium	High	High	High
Credit Card	Low (if repaid within credit period)	High	High	High
Trade Credit	Low	High	High	High
Retained Profit	Low	High	High	High
Banks	Low	Medium	High	High
Business Angels	Low	Medium	Shared	Shared
Venture Capital	Low	Low	Shared	Shared
IPO	Low	Low	Shared	Shared

Figure 12.2: Debt / Equity matrix

11. Life Cycle Finance

The availability and attractiveness of the different sources of finance change through the business life cycle. The listing aligns well with the availability of funds for fledgling start up companies. For example, a new venture without a track record is unlikely to attract venture capital investment and, conversely, an established company is unlikely to ask family and friends for a major injection of cash.

Figure 12.3 graphicly outlines the typical sources of finance as the company progresses through the business life cycle. This will help the entrepreneur focus on the types of finance to be pursued while progressing through the company's different phases. In the initial phases the entrepreneur should focus on networking, personal funds, family and friends, as they are unlikely to attract venture capital or an IPO. In the rapid growth and maturity phases, the entrepreneur should focus on venture capital and an IPO, because an established company is unlikely to ask family and friends for finance.

Concept Phase	Start-up Phase	Survival Phase	Growth Phase	Maturity Phase	Declining Phase
Networking					
Personal Savings					
Family					
Friends					
Credit Card					
	Trade Credit				
		Retained Profit			
	Banks (Overdraft / Loans)				
			Business Angels		
			Venture Capital		
			IPO		

Figure 12.3: Life Cycle Finance (note the distinction between the sources of finance in the start up phases compared to the sources of finance in the growth and maturity phases)

cosmic mba series

12. Business Plan

At some point, as ideas and opportunities evolve into marketable products, the entrepreneur needs to formalise his approach with a coherent business plan that encapsulates short and long term estimates on paper. The business plan should not only ensure the entrepreneurial venture is feasible, but also confirm there is a market for the product, and that the venture is making the best use of the entrepreneur's time and resources.

The business plan structure includes a number of sections which outline what the entrepreneur intends to do with respect to; what, when, how and why. Business plans tend to follow a standard format that gives a clear overview of a new venture in a format that bank managers prefer.

Executive Summary:
- overview of the new venture
- outline the type of business
- identify the market
- outline the business potential and sales forecast
- profit forecast
- how much money needs to be raised
- return on investment
- risk assessment.

Business Description of the Product:
- description of what the product or service offers
- what is different or unique about the product or service
- briefly outline the competition
- how the product will be developed, what new products are in the pipeline
- what patents have been applied for.

Company Structure:
- past employment and business experience
- CV of team members
- strengths and weaknesses
- identify stakeholders, particularly close links with suppliers and contractors.

Sales and Marketing:
- likely customer profile
- market size, growth (past, present, future)
- niche market opportunities
- competitors: who are they, their size, market share, possible response to the product, and price strategy

- how will the product be sold and distributed; Internet, direct mail, telephone selling, distributors, retailers
- promotion, advertising, sales brochure.

Manufacturing and Distribution:
- location
- equipment and manufacturing facilities
- build-method and feasibility study
- suppliers
- warehouse, stock control (JIT)
- distribution
- shipping, transport and vehicles.

Financial Statement:
- estimate set up costs
- estimate operational costs
- forecast sales
- payback period
- breakeven analysis
- cashflow statement
- return on investment (ROI) and discounted cash flow.

Risk Management:
- risk analysis
- risk response
- disaster recovery.

The business plan pulls together all the key topics. These are further developed in my book on *Small Business Entrepreneur*.

Exercises:

1. Discuss how you have networked to gain the free use of resources to start a new venture.

2. Discuss how you have borrowed funds from family and friends - what were the terms?

3. Discuss how you have used your credit card and trade credit to obtain a short term loan.

Instructor's Manual: An Instructor's Manual is available with additional exercises and case studies, see *<www.knowledgezone.net>*.

13
Managing Growth

LEARNING OUTCOMES - enables the reader to:

Show how company growth can be presented on the lifecycle graph.

Develop the six phases of the lifecycle.

Explain the success-disaster scenario.

Discuss the differences between rapid growth companies and lifestyle companies.

Who would have thought the worst thing that could happen to an entrepreneur is that they become successful? Unfortunately this is true! When some small companies hit the accelerator and suddenly grow very fast, instead of laughing all the way to the bank, their growth turns into a production nightmare. The irony is that the very leadership style that established the company in the start up phase, might actually lead to a **success-disaster** in the growth phase.

Managing growth is the achilles' heel for the typical entrepreneur. While the company is small the entrepreneur can manage everything in his head on a day-to-day basis but, with rapid growth, the entrepreneur's ad hoc leadership style needs to change to a more formalised management approach to enable effective planning and control. And here-in lies the problem - entrepreneurs, by their very nature, are motivated by opportunities, freedom, risk and profit - whereas managers are motivated by resources, delegation and security.

Small businesses generally consist of the founder and their partner, and a few employees. By contrast, rapid growth companies create plenty of employment and suck in large amounts of resources and funding, which ultimately expands the local economy. This is why rapid growth companies are so important to the economy and the darling of the stock market, particularly for an IPO (initial public offering). But, the reality is, rapid growth companies only account for 5% of the start up companies; of the others, 50% fail within three years and the rest are slow growing lifestyle companies.

As companies grow they pass through a number of distinct phases. Figure 13.1 subdivides company growth into six phases - from the cradle to the grave. Each phase has its own distinct characteristics, challenges and opportunities which need to be considered, planned and controlled.

1. **Concept Phase:** Considers ideas and opportunities - this is where the feasibility study would be carried out.

2. **Start Up Phase:** Sets up the business and starts offering the product or service to the market.

3. **Survival Phase:** This is the reality test - is the business going to develop a trading profit before the seed money runs out?

4. **Growth Phase:** Lifestyle companies go for sustained growth from retained profits, while growth companies go for rapid expansion requiring a large injection of funds and an upgrade of their systems.

5. **Maturity Phase:** Company growth often expands into bureaucracy and red tape which stifles the very innovation that underpinned the company's original growth. Management begins to replace business leadership, as they prefer to keep tried and tested products rather than risk investment in new product development.

6. **Declining Phase:** Failure to respond to new technology leaves the company with obsolete products and declining sales. The company is seriously in need of entrepreneurial shock treatment, or it will end up as a candidate for takeover or closure.

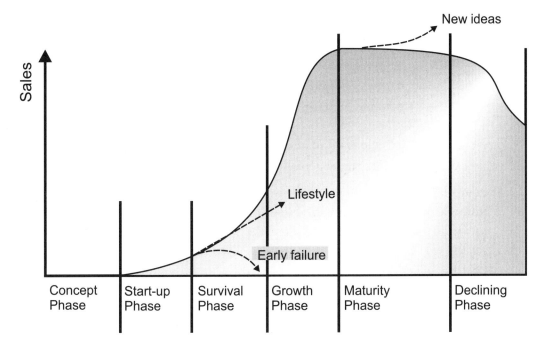

Figure 13.1: New Venture Growth Phases

1. Concept Phase (1)

The concept phase is often overlooked in other publications. This might be because it is the preparation phase before the company actually starts trading. This is the time for the entrepreneur to kick ideas around, search for opportunities and test their feasibility.

The entrepreneur should consider the wider implications of leaving secure employment for the uncertain prospects of running a business - particularly with respect to family and income. It is also the time to identify what new skills and expertise might be needed and attend short courses to build up a skills base.

"If only I'd known what was involved I would never have started". How often have we heard that comment? Although a business plan and feasibility study might sound like a damper, if it prevents the entrepreneur charging headlong into potential disasters and white elephants, it will be well worth the effort. The business plan will at least provide a framework to plan ahead and a sound basis on which to make strategic decisions.

There is usually a **trigger** encouraging the entrepreneur to start a new venture (see *Who Wants to be an Entrepreneur?* chapter). Some entrepreneurs wait on the starting blocks for an opportunity to get them going - this way they can hit the ground running. While the entrepreneur is exploring possible products or services to offer, as much ground work as possible should be done. Consider the following:

- develop and test the prototype product
- conduct market research to assess the market potential and competition
- consider financial requirements and sources of finance
- consider possible premises, build-method, machinery requirements and distribution
- identify possible team members, suppliers and contractors
- develop business management systems.

The output from this phase should be a coherent business plan and a healthy dose of enthusiasm, determination and commitment to make-it-happen.

2. Start up Phase (2)

Most entrepreneurs start from humble beginnings with a simple organisation structure – usually just the entrepreneur and their partner. Some companies start slowly and build-up speed as the company establishes itself, while others start with a big bang because of the nature of their business - opening a shop for example.

At the start up there will be high excitement and enthusiasm fuelled by finally getting the business off the ground - the thrill of the first customer. But, as the reality of the business kicks in, having learnt what is involved, the entrepreneur must develop business skills to be able to respond to peoples' needs, expectations and reactions.

Family and friends might be willing helpers at the beginning, happily following instructions to help get the business started but, next time the entrepreneur needs help, he should consider paid employees from outside the family circle.

There will be many challenges facing the fledgling business, because the entrepreneur will not have the same knowledge or information as competitors. The entrepreneur's credit rating will inevitably be on the bottom rung of the ladder - making it more difficult and expensive to raise funds. And, as a new venture, the entrepreneur will have to establish credibility with the customers.

A small team working closely together enables internal communication to be frequent and informal. Initially there will probably be a high sense of confusion and apprehension regarding the company's goals and objectives, and even concerns about the survival of the company, but there will also be enthusiasm to work long hours to get the job done and beat the competition.

Human life cycle - spot the entrepreneur!

3. Survival Phase (3)

The survival phase is the viability test - is the venture going to develop sufficient income to pay the bills before the seed money runs out? As the start up capital is progressively consumed, the key questions are;

- is the company attracting sufficient customers - particularly repeat business?
- is the cash flow generating positive working capital - is income greater than expenditure?
- are the products making a trading profit - is the selling price greater than the manufacturing costs?

The survival phase is a minefield for new ventures - many companies do not make it past this phase. If the small business is not attracting sufficient customers to be financially viable, then radical action needs to be taken quickly before the seed money runs out. This happened to Anita Roddick when she bought a residential hotel in Littlehampton and turned it into a bed and breakfast place (this was before Anita opened the Body Shop).

'Everything was going fine until the summer season ended. Suddenly there were no more customers and we found ourselves saddled with a huge empty house and horrendous maintenance costs. We realized we were going to go bankrupt unless we did something and did it quickly. What we did was to turn half the house back into a residential hotel. That saved us and taught us a lesson valuable to all budding entrepreneurs: when you make a mistake, you have to face up to the fact and take immediate steps to change course.'

Anita Roddick had a similar experience with a restaurant which she had to change from a stylish Italian cuisine with no patrons to a packed American hamburger joint with rock music - *'the effect was miraculous'*. With these experiences under her belt, three years later she opened the first Body Shop.

If the new venture is not performing as hoped for, the entrepreneur will begin to question why are they putting themselves through this torture, particularly if they could be earning more money in a secure job working for someone else, rather than working on their own doing things the hard way.

4. Growth Phase (4)

As new ventures make it through the start up and survival phases this confirms they have established a niche market, formed a solid customer base and built a sound reputation for the product. This also implies the company is trading profitably and the venture is now in a position to consider its future direction - possible expansion and growth. There are many reasons why an entrepreneur might want to grow their business or, in some cases, have growth thrust upon them:

- expand to meet growing demand for the product (thank you very much)
- restrict competition (perhaps the most important reason), because if the entrepreneur cannot meet the demand, they are simply inviting competitors into the market they have established
- expand the production facility to achieve economies of scale - with bigger production runs the entrepreneur should be able to reduce the unit cost
- create local employment
- enrich the stakeholders and venture capitalists.

There are two distinct growth strategies the entrepreneur can use to expand their business:

- sustainable growth - as a lifestyle company using retained profits
- rapid growth - requiring a large injection of capital.

Lifestyle Companies: Lifestyle companies confound the typical perception that all entrepreneurs want to get rich (see *Who Wants to be an Entrepreneur?* chapter). Not all entrepreneurial companies grow and generate great wealth, some just tick along, maybe as a family unit. The motivation for these entrepreneurs is not growth and riches, but satisfying work that generates sufficient income to live a comfortable way of life.

Lifestyle companies typically stay small and independent, and are run by their founders. Their growth is usually incremental, as internal funds become available from retained profits, and they grow to a size the entrepreneur feels is manageable. This is called sustainable growth.

A lifestyle business would typically be the entrepreneur's main source of income, their wealth, and perhaps even their pension. The prospect of rapid growth would concern them, because they could lose control, leaving them with nothing. One of the triggers to start their business in the first place is usually to gain as much independence and control over their destiny as possible, so handing control back to others, even if there is the prospect of rapid growth, is not an option.

Growth Companies: In contrast to the lifestyle companies, growth companies go for rapid expansion, and aim to become a leading player in their field. This will almost certainly require a large external injection of funds to finance the marketing effort to create the demand, and funds to increase the production facilities to meet the demand. There are basically two classic ways to grow a company;

- horizontal growth
- vertical growth.

Horizontal growth is achieved by selling more products to more customers. This can be achieved in a number of ways:

- Establishing new uses for the product, for example, rebranding Lucozade from a convalescence drink to a sports drink.
- Developing new products for the customer base, for example, a publisher would produce new book titles.
- Attracting new customers locally by advertising and lowering prices.
- Exporting to new geographical areas in your home country and overseas.
- Selling globally through the Internet.
- Finding other companies to pay you for the privilege of using your creative ideas and selling your product - franchising, licensing, rights and royalties.

Vertical growth is achieved by expanding the company's activities up and down the product's supply chain - from raw materials to manufacture, and from distribution to retailing. The parts of the supply chain that the entrepreneur can expand into obviously depend on where the entrepreneur's product is positioned in the supply chain.

- Many oil companies have achieved nearly full vertical penetration of their supply chain, up stream to the oil wells and down stream to the retail filling stations. The oil companies own and operate oil rigs, super tankers, oil refineries and filling stations and, in some locations, the motorway filling stations have expanded into mini shopping malls.
- A company can expand upstream to gain control of the supply of raw materials. This can be achieved by acquiring the present suppliers, or by starting their own company to supply the raw materials. For example, Henry Ford did this when he bought a cattle farm to guarantee the supply of leather to cover the car seats.
- A company can expand downstream to gain control of the distribution and the retailing of the product. With Internet sales the entrepreneur might be able to cut out the middleman and sell the product direct to the customer, as <www.Amazon.com> does with books.

- Supermarkets expand vertically by including a high percentage of their own 'no name brand' products.
- Growth can be achieved through partnerships, alliances and acquisitions with other companies in the supply chain. This can occur particularly with companies that have a marketable product, established client base, skilled workers in the field of interest and have working relationships with suppliers and customers.

Expanding the business up or down the supply chain will not necessarily increase the number of products sold, but it will increase the entrepreneur's percentage income from each sale. In practice, growth is usually achieved by a combination of both horizontal and vertical expansion.

Growing Pains: Rapid growth usually requires some major changes in the entrepreneur's leadership style and the company's management systems so that they can plan and control larger volumes of the product. Otherwise there might be some unpleasant surprises, not least the contradictory sounding **success-disaster** scenario.

A success-disaster can happen when the sales and marketing team hits the sweet spot and demand for the product suddenly takes off. The entrepreneur's knee-jerk reaction is usually to try and gear up production to meet the demand. But if the manufacturing and distribution cannot keep up, this will create shortages and stressed out workers.

The product shortages will cause the help desk to get swamped with enquiries from angry customers. The knock-on effect of the inability to deliver will result in the company developing a bad reputation with its customers, which might allow its competitors into the very market the entrepreneur has personally pioneered and developed.

In the attempt to meet demand the employees will be over worked and be getting increasingly frustrated which could result in some key people actually leaving the company. These people will be replaced by new workers who will not know the ropes - this has the potential of creating a vicious spiral.

The financial side could be even worse as the company builds up stock and has to wait for the inflow of income. Without financial support, the upfront costs will create negative cash flow which could drive the company into liquidation.

The tragedy of this scenario is that it usually does end in disaster - the company simply spirals out of control. The best way to survive the success-disaster is to try to prevent it happening in the first place by being prepared to manage growth with effective management skills and production controls.

Communication Breakdown: As companies grow and expand, communication is one of the first management systems to come under pressure. Due to the entrepreneur's increasing workload he will not be able to spend as much time informally contacting people as he used to. If a more formal communication system is not established, this lack of communication can quickly lead to;

- disruptive rumors about changing roles
- new employees are unsure of what to do and need guidance.

These minor problems soon magnify leading to chaos, frustration and ultimately a loss of productivity. This is where the entrepreneur needs to strike a balance and move from a naturally casual way of communicating to a more structured communication plan with scheduled meetings and even memos.

Production Quality: As the demand for the product increases so the methods of production management need to change. Short ad-hoc production runs to meet demand need to change to longer planned production runs to achieve larger volumes and economies of scale. This will require JIT raw material procurement, warehousing, increased stock control, increased quality control, increased distribution, increased staff, and to accommodate the expansion, probably bigger premises as well.

To meet the increased demand the production department might be tempted to cut corners to increase output - this runs the risk of mistakes and lower quality. This route will come back to haunt them if it leads to rejections, rework and an increase in customer service complaints.

Production can also be increased by outsourcing and offshoring. This has the added benefit of enabling the entrepreneur to focus on his core business. Although outsourcing and offshoring might reduce the entrepreneur's workload, the subcontractors will still need to be closely managed. Otherwise this could lead to quality control problems, and now there is the further complication of the products being in a third party's factory which may well be in another country.

Cash Flow: Growth companies will need large amounts of investment to develop new product designs, conduct marketing promotions, implement management systems, install manufacturing facilities and buy new premises. Ploughing the profits back into the company will give a healthy sustainable growth rate (say +/- 10%) but, for rapid growth (say +/- 100%), the company will almost certainly require a large injection of outside funds.

To expand the business the entrepreneur will need to build up a stock of materials and products in the supply chain (called **stocking**). The time it takes to

recover these costs gives an indication of the amount that needs to be budgeted for the stocking costs. The converse is also true - as a company destocks it does wonders for the cash flow.

As the number of financial transactions increase, the accounting procedures must change from **shoe-box accounting** to a more formal integrated accounting system, linking procurement, wages, materials, operation costs, office costs and tax.

Rapid growth will make cash flow forecasting more difficult. There will be greater fluctuations, with an increased risk of negative cash flow as upfront costs could exceed payments. Bank overdrafts will need to be organised well in advance.

The inability to finance negative cash flow could be the final nail in the coffin facing the rapidly growing company. The entrepreneur might have calculated his estimates accurately to make a good profit margin but, if the company cannot hang in there until the funds start flowing in, it will end up with a cash flow disaster. This is why financial controls are essential.

The cash flow wave

People: As demand for the product increases there will almost certainly be a need to employ more people to do the work. Forming teams is not a natural trait for entrepreneurs who are intrinsically egotistical and independent. But if the entrepreneur wants the company to grow the number of employees must be increased, otherwise the company will just hit the wall faster. Addressing the resource issue successfully is another important entrepreneurial trait - they must be able to link the opportunity and market with the resources and implementation.

During the start up phases the company attracts people who are happy to follow the entrepreneur's leadership but, in the growth phase, the entrepreneur needs to hire people who know how to develop and manage larger production facilities.

As the company grows the '*old boys*' will probably expect to be promoted into the new positions, but what if they are not able to up-skill to meet the new challenges? The entrepreneur might have some hard decisions to make balancing loyalty with bringing experienced workers into the management team.

With an expanding workforce, the once-tight-knit team might feel invaded by the newcomers. This might threaten the very entrepreneurial spirit that founded the company in the first place. Although management systems are necessary to plan and control the expanding workload, it is essential to keep the entrepreneurial spirit alive.

The start up company is very personal to the entrepreneur - it is their baby - so bringing more people into the company, although it helps to spread the workload, also means the entrepreneur must share control.

A company's problems and solutions tend to change markedly as the number of employees and the volumes of sales increase. Problems of co-ordination and communication magnify, new functions emerge, levels in the management hierarchy increase, and jobs become more inter-related. As the company expands, the entrepreneur will no longer be able to be involved in every decision.

Leadership: Entrepreneurs are masters at spotting opportunities but, with rapid growth, they might not have the time and resources to attend to all the work they have generated - and so be spread a bit thin. They might have difficulty finishing one job before being distracted by another, resulting in an increasing number of unfinished jobs.

As the company expands the entrepreneur needs to change from a leader of a small team to a manager of a large production facility. This will require knowledge about the efficiencies of manufacturing and production management. An increased number of employees cannot be managed exclusively through informal communication. New employees might not be as motivated by an

intense dedication to the product or organisation as the original team members. Additional capital must be secured, and new accounting procedures are needed for financial control. The company's founding entrepreneur will be burdened with unwanted management responsibilities. The entrepreneur might long for the '*good old days*' and try to act as he did in the past. Conflict among hassled leaders might emerge and intensify.

If the entrepreneur cannot manage the changing work environment a **crisis in leadership** will occur, which often signifies the onset of revolutionary change within the company. Who will lead the company out of the confusion and solve the managerial problems confronting the company? A strong manager is needed - one who has the necessary knowledge and skills to introduce new production management and business management techniques.

Management Teams: The management of a rapidly growing company requires a range of different skills which any one manager is unlikely to have - but a balanced team could have these required skills. The track record of successful new ventures supports this theory. Growth companies are more likely to be successful if they are managed by a management team rather than an individual entrepreneur. It is for this reason that venture capital firms prefer to invest in management teams (buy-ins and buy-outs) rather than a business per se.

Attracting a strong management team to a start up company can be a problem. How do you tempt successful managers to leave secure jobs and face the risks associated with a business start up? The answer might be by offering them a share of the business, but now the entrepreneur will have to give some of their business away!

Entrepreneurs with previous managerial experience are more likely to be associated with growth companies. This is because they bring with them both managerial experience (they know the ropes) and market understanding. They also know their worth, which will create salary expectations which can only be satisfied by a growth business. Middle-aged managers also bring experience, credibility, financial resources and staying power.

Delegation: During the start up phase the entrepreneur will be involved with most of the tasks but, as the workload increases, the entrepreneur cannot do it all himself, so work will have to be delegated and control give to other team members. Skilful delegation is the key to effective leadership and growth. Through delegation the leader (entrepreneur) can improve team efficiency, develop employee ability and contribute to the growth of the company. There are four basic elements to delegating:

- assign a task to an employee (make them feel responsible for its completion)
- allocate sufficient authority so the employee can command the resources necessary to accomplish the task
- gain commitment and confirm the employee wants to do the task
- monitor performance and give support - do not leave the employee on their own to founder (there is a delicate balance between interfering and taking control, and letting the employee learn from mistakes).

Sir Richard Branson, head of the Virgin Group, delegates at the director level of each of his companies. This enables each Virgin company to make its own decisions on a day-to-day basis as they strive to achieve agreed goals.

5. Maturity Phase (5)

As growth companies expand and become firmly established in their market they consolidate and mature, and tend to invest their capital and effort into improving and optimizing their current offerings, rather than investing in developing completely new products.

In times of great profitability it is difficult to persuade successful companies to divert resources from their successful money earners into exploring risky new product development. With sound management systems in place a mature company should be able to enjoy stable growth, but be watching out for radical changes in technology and market requirements.

6. Declining Phase (6)

Mature companies that fail to develop new products will eventually be overtaken by new technology and changing market requirements. As mature companies continue to rely on a few tried and tested products that have seen them right in the past, they will find themselves clinging on to increasingly obsolete products. This is the classic 'cash cow' situation where the company continues to milk a successful product and not reinvest in new technology.

This is the CEO's last chance to make an emergency, SOS call for an entrepreneur to kick start and revitalise the company in a new direction before the vultures start circling around the ailing company.

Exercises:

1. Successful entrepreneurs are said to know their strengths and weaknesses, and bring in experts to cover their weaknesses. Discuss how this applies to you.

2. For an entrepreneur's company to grow, he needs to know how to build a bigger company. Discuss how you address growth.

3. Consider the growth life cycle (figure 13.1) and link a company you know to each of the phases.

Instructor's Manual: An Instructor's Manual is available with additional exercises and case studies, see <*www.knowledgezone.net*>.

"....It's an email from the office - they're working overtime...."

14
Risk
Management

LEARNING OUTCOMES - enables the reader to:

Explain the classic risk management models.

Understand the difference between perceived risk and real risk and the influence this has on peoples attitude.

Discuss the effect internal locus of control, self-confidence, optimism and courage have on people's attitude to risk.

Discuss the implications of failure and bankruptcy.

Entrepreneurs are usually stereotyped as foolhardy risk takers, almost by definition, marching into new ventures where *angels fear to tread*. They are seen by many as adventurers, laying everything on the line, moving from one make or break deal to another. They are even said to occasionally gamble their homes to finance their next venture.

To understand how entrepreneurs deal with risk, failure and rejection goes right to the heart of entrepreneurship. Although the management techniques provide a structured methodology for entrepreneurs to follow, to really understand their approach to risk one has to look at their personal traits and perceptions (these are developed later in the chapter).

There are a number of management techniques that help the entrepreneur to select new ventures, assess risk and develop a strategy for the future. The risk management model (see figure 14.1) helps to identify the risks and develop appropriate responses. While the twin techniques of problem-solving and decision-making (see figure 14.2) helps to provide the best technical solutions which the stakeholders will collectively support.

Dealing With Rejection: Implementing opportunities and setting up new ventures, by their very nature, change the status quo. Some stakeholders will see these changes as an improvement and support them, while other stakeholders might prefer things to stay as they are, and so reject the new venture.

Most sales people have to deal with rejection everyday - it is the nature of their business. For example, when Chay Blyth was promoting his round the world sailing challenge, it was reported he had to contact 17 companies to get just one sponsor. So for the unknown entrepreneurs setting up a new venture with a new product, they might well have to work with an even less attractive success ratio.

Entrepreneurs, in their drive to promote and establish new products and new ventures, will almost certainly have to deal with rejection, in which case, managers who are scared of rejection are unlikely to start a new venture, and therefore are unlikely to make it as an entrepreneur.

Risk adverse managers make their decisions based on the fear of what could go wrong, while proactive entrepreneurs make their decisions based on their vision of what could go right.

1. Risk Management Model

The risk management model focuses on the risks and uncertainties which might prevent a new venture achieving its business objectives. The model identifies the risks, then quantifies them with respect to frequency and impact, then develops responses to eliminate, mitigate, deflect, or accept the risks (with a contingency plan).

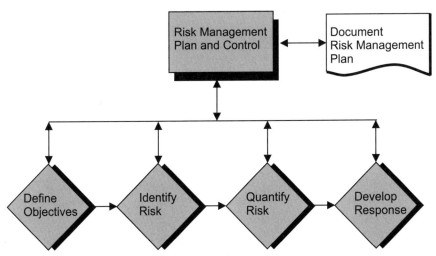

Figure 14.1: Risk Management Model (for more information see my book *Project Management Planning and Control Techniques*)

2. Problem-Solving and Decision-Making Model

The twin problem-solving and decision-making techniques are key management tools for developing and implementing the entrepreneur's strategy.

The problem-solving spiral is used to find the best technical solutions to solve the identified problem. By repeating the loop many times the entrepreneur progressively converges on a number of optimum solutions.

These solutions are then passed over to the decision-making spiral where the focus is on gaining collective support to accept one or more of the solutions and to commit company resources to implement them.

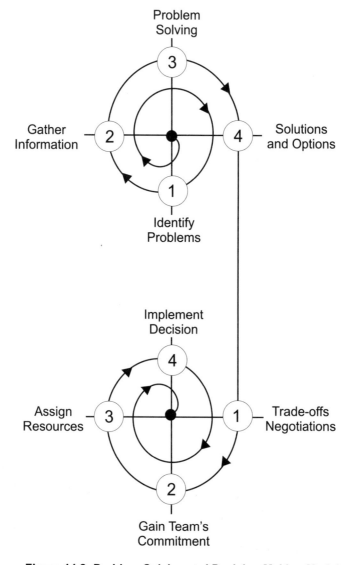

Figure 14.2: Problem-Solving and Decision Making Model

3. Perceived Risk

These risk management models are based on the assumption that we are able to accurately identify the risks and are able to adequately respond to the risks - and here-in lies the problem.

When we identify a risk it is usually based on our perception of the risk - and this can vary from person to person, and further vary within each person from time to time. This is because our perception of risk changes with our experience and knowledge of the situation. It is further influenced by the amount of information and the accuracy of the information we have on the situation, and by the time we have to consider all the trade-offs, and make the decision.

If you are doing a job for the first time (manoeuvring a yacht into a marina berth for example), you are likely to air on the cautious side. Whereas someone who is doing the job everyday would consider it routine. The person's experience and knowledge of the job, as in this example, will obviously influence their perception of the risk.

If you have just had a good run on the stock market you are more likely to consider investing in riskier start up ventures as you feel you have acquired the Midas touch. But if your stocks have just been dragged down by a bear run, you will probably become a more cautious investor, even consider putting your money under your mattress!!

This attitude to risk can be shown on the risk perception scale. If the real inherent risk is in the middle of the scale, then someone who is risk adverse might perceive the risk as being far greater than the actual risk. While an overconfident risk positive person might underestimate the actual risk. So with these two extreme perceptions of the same risk, the responses are likely to be very different.

4. Risk Response

The situation is further complicated by people responding differently even when they have the same perception of the risk - that is they are at the same point on the risk perception scale.

It is often said that entrepreneurs take risks, and accept failure and rejection in their stride - this is misleading because it only looks at one side of the coin. What is more accurate is to say that entrepreneurs develop a number of traits for managing and coping with problems and this influences the way they respond to risk.

5. Internal Locus of Control

Entrepreneurs with a strong internal locus of control believe their lives, their destiny and their successes are determined by their own actions and not by the actions of others. If they fail, they accept that it is because of their own actions. So, by analysing their actions and addressing their shortcomings, entrepreneurs believe they will be successful next time round.

It follows that if entrepreneurs feel they are in control of their lives, it is reasonable to suggest that they also feel in control of their risks - if they have a problem they can fix it.

The opposite - external locus of control - applies to people who believe their lives, their destiny and their successes are determined by the actions of others. They expect other people to make decisions for them and, if there is a problem, they expect other people to fix it. They believe in fate, and would be inclined to check their star signs and tea leaves before making a decision. They would not last long as an entrepreneur! It is this attitude that makes people believe that the world owes them a living - while true entrepreneurs know they advance from their own efforts.

6. Self-Confidence

Entrepreneurs believe in themselves, they are self-confident and know they can do the job. This is reflected in their decision-making. Research shows that entrepreneurs are statistically more **confident** of their decisions than other managers, even though the entrepreneurs decisions are no better than other managers and, in many cases, are actually wrong.

When entrepreneurs are decisive it makes other people believe they are right - which in turn helps to make the decision right! In many cases the ability to make a quick decision between A or B (two similar products) is better than a protracted lengthy debate to select the best option. A quick decision enables the entrepreneur to take advantage of an opportunity which will not last forever, and could be lost or reduced if he has to wait for the outcome of a lengthy detailed feasibility study.

When entrepreneurs make a mistake they have the self-confidence and persistence to try again and again until they get it right. Persistence, determination and stubbornness are traits that keep entrepreneurs going when they hit rejections and problems - this is why entrepreneurs are often said to **refuse to accept failure**. In fact, the entrepreneur might know that they are wrong, but are going to '*stick to their guns*' and make their solution work anyway.

7. Optimistic

Couple internal locus of control and self-confidence with a healthy dose of optimism, and we start to see why entrepreneurs are prepared to make decisions. Not only do they believe they can do the job in the first place, and fix any problems that might recur, but they also believe everything will work out for the best anyway.

Entrepreneurs are born optimists having a strong expectation that despite setbacks and frustrations, things will turn out right in the end - their glass is always half full!

People who are optimistic and have a strong locus of internal control, see failure and rejection as being due to something that can be changed so that they can succeed next time round. While pessimists take the blame for their failure, ascribing it to some lasting personal characteristic they are helpless to change.

These differing explanations have profound implications on how people respond to failure. For example, the reaction to a disappointment such as being turned down for a job, the optimist will respond actively and positively, by formulating a plan of action - seeking out help and advice. They see the rejection as a short term setback, and something that can be put right.

People who are pessimistic and have an external locus of control, by contrast, will react to a job rejection by assuming it is due to some personal fault that will always plague them and cannot be put right. They feel there is nothing they can do to improve things, so do nothing about the problem - which means the problem is likely to reoccur - setting up a negative spiral.

In the case of a new venture, the entrepreneur will conduct a problem-solving exercise and a risk assessment as any manager would do, but what they do with the information makes all the difference. The entrepreneur will take the optimistic view and believe the new venture will develop as planned. The pessimist, by contrast, will take the negative view and see the venture as a series of risks and uncertainties which can only lead to failure.

"....as I was saying, I've got a good book on risk management......oh**!!?...."

8. Courage

Even if all the problem-solving calculations and feedback are positive, it still takes courage to take the plunge and commit resources to start a new venture, particularly when the entrepreneur's assets and reputation are on the line.

Obsolete technology

"....I'm still holding on...."

Managing a business that is changing the status quo will always encounter problems and resistance to change. Confronting these problems takes courage - it is always easier to walk away. Ironically doing nothing might well make the situation worse! As discussed in the *Do We Need Entrepreneurs* chapter, if businesses are not developing new products they will be increasingly clinging on to obsolete technology. It takes courage for the entrepreneur to stand and fight for their product but, by doing so, they will also earn respect from the other players.

9. Risk Shift

It might surprise you to note that most of us quite often let other people make our risk management decisions for us - most of us are like reef fish, following the crowd. However, this might not actually be a bad thing because there is research to suggest that the larger the sample the more accurate the response. For example, in the '*Who Wants to Be a Millionaire*" programme, when a contestant asks the audience, the majority answer is usually correct. And of-course this is the basis of our democratic society.

There are, however, situations when risk shift can lead people into trouble. Consider a group of people out walking in the mountains. If it starts to cloud over and rain heavily a few people might think of turning back because they are concerned about getting lost and rising river levels. If they look at the rest of the group who appear to be happily carrying on and decide to follow the crowd, this means they have made their decision based on what the others are doing - in effect shifting their decision to be made by the other people.

By investing in a managed fund you are effectively giving your money to someone else to invest as they see fit. You are assuming that they have better knowledge and understanding of the market.

10. Failure and Bankruptcy

Failure and bankruptcy are not the financial, personal and social disasters they used to be. In fact, bankruptcy has become almost common place - even Donald Trump filed for Chapter 11 protection while portraying himself as the model CEO in The *Apprentice*. A number of the large American airline companies seem to permanently live in Chapter 11 protection and yet still continue to trade as normal.

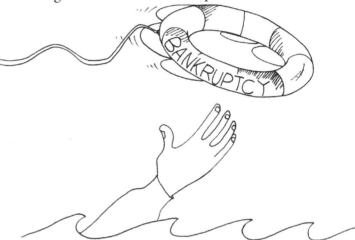

Statistics indicate that the typical entrepreneur will have a number of business failures under his belt before experiencing true success - even Henry Ford failed twice before becoming the largest car manufacturer in the world.

With such a high rate of failure it is therefore imperative that the entrepreneur limits the downside and his exposure to risk. In an interview, Richard Branson explained that when he is offered a new venture, he checks the downside and asks how much he would be committing if the venture went belly-up. To survive long term, it is important the entrepreneur has an exit strategy and knows how to cut his losses and get out. It is like abandoning a sinking ship for a secure liferaft - to live and fight another day.

Exercises:

1. Give an example of how the risk management model (figure 14.1) can be used on one of your ventures. Answer the question by setting up a proforma to identify and list: objective, risk and response.

2. Give an example of how the problem-solving and decision-making techniques (figure 14.2) can be used on one of your ventures.

3. How do the entrepreneurial traits of internal locus of control, self-confidence, optimism, and courage apply to you?

Instructor's Manual: An Instructor's Manual is available with additional exercises and case studies, see *<www.knowledgezone.net>*.

Glossary of Terms

Body of Knowledge: The body of knowledge (of a profession) identifies and describes the generally accepted practices for which there is widespread consensus of their value and usefulness, and also establishes a common lexicon of terms and expressions used within the profession (entrepreneurship in this case).

Brand: A brand is everything that makes up how the business and product are viewed by others, particularly the customers. The brand is created by the way the business is promoted and advertised, and through its business name and company logo.

Breakeven Point: This is the number of products the company needs to sell to cover the set up costs - after this point the company starts to make a profit.

Brainstorming: A group method of generating a flood of creative ideas and novel solutions.

Business Angel: A wealthy private investor who provides small amounts of their own capital to seed entrepreneurial ventures. They also offer support and guidance to help the entrepreneur establish a management system.

Business Plan: The business plan is an all encompassing document which outlines how the company will produce the product and confirm the new venture is feasible.

Cash Flow: The money that flows in and out of the business - typically presented as a monthly snap shot.

Competitive Advantage: Companies achieve competitive advantage over their competitors by offering a better product with better features, by being first to market or by offering their products at a lower selling price.

Creative Ideas: Is the use of ingenuity and imagination to create a novel approach or a unique solution to a problem.

Decision-Making: Decision-making focuses on gaining the collective support of the team members to commit company resources to implement an agreed course of action.

Enterprise: A bold undertaking or business activity which shows initiative and foresight.

Entrepreneur: A person who spots an opportunity and co-ordinates resources to make-it-happen.

Equity: The value of a business owned by the shareholders after all the debts and liabilities have been taken into account.

Equity Investor: Funds provided for company growth in exchange for a shareholding in the venture.

Exit Strategy: How an investor plans to withdraw from a business, particularly when it is making a loss.

Feasibility Study: Ensures all aspects of the new venture are feasible, confirming that the product can be manufactured, the product will work, and there is a market for the product. Most importantly, confirming the new venture will make the best use of the company's resources.

Franchise: The franchisee buys the rights from the franchisor to operate an outlet of an established business (such as McDonalds). The franchisee's fee is usually made up of an annual payment and percentage of turnover. Besides buying the rights, the payment includes management systems, equipment, training and support.

Growth Phase: Small businesses pass through a number of recognisable phases, beginning with the set up phase and the survival phase, followed by the growth phase where the company rapidly grows as the demand for the product increases.

Hypnagogia: A state of deeply relaxed consciousness, between sleep and waking-up, during which flashes of inspiration and creative insight often appear. Researchers have found these transition periods to be quite short, seldom more than ten minutes.

Incubator: A science park or business centre which helps to develop fledgling start up businesses until they can operate successfully on their own. The incubator provides access to shared facilities, support and networking.

Innovation: Is more than a flash of inspiration, it is the systematic development and implementation of the creative idea.

IPO: Initial Public Offering is the sale of company equity usually through the stock market.

Lateral Thinking: Method of solving problems indirectly or by apparently illogical methods - when you hit a problem you go around it.

Lifestyle Entrepreneur: The balance between earning mega-bucks in the city and having a meaningful lifestyle - perhaps in the country. A lifestyle company will typically stay small and independent. It will depend heavily on its founders, and grow incrementally as internal funds become available.

Marketing Plan: A document outlining marketing objectives, strategies and activities, usually part of the business plan.

Market Research: A process to ensure the entrepreneur is offering the right product to the right people. Basic market research tries to ensure there is a demand for the product and market potential with respect to the competition.

Mentor: An experienced business person (often previously an entrepreneur) who offers their advice (usually gratis) to start up companies.

Negotiation: The process of resolving differences between two or more parties, preferably using the win-win collaborative approach.

Networking: Through their contacts the entrepreneur uses the back door (beg, borrow and befriend) to gain access to ideas, information and resources they need to make their product and gain competitive advantage.

Niche Market: A non-mainstream market, usually small and requiring specialised skills.

Offshoring: Outsourcing work to an overseas company (typically 'back office' work and call-centres to India and manufacturing to China).

Opportunities: Business opportunities are ideas and changes which will give the entrepreneur competitive advantage over their competitors.

Outsourcing: Using an external supplier to make part or all of your products, or to take over admin jobs such as processing the wages - usually non-core activities, and the aim is to reduce operational costs and capital expenditure.

Paradigm Shift: Science is not necessarily a smooth transition of incremental inventions, but rather a series of revolutions, expressed as paradigm shifts. A paradigm means a set of assumptions, methods, and models that define the change.

Problem-Solving: Generating a number of technical solutions to solve a problem, which is then handed over to the decision-making function to select the solution which enjoys the widest support and commitment from the team members.

Product: Goods or services the entrepreneur intends to sell.

Project Management: Management techniques used to plan and control change, particularly implementing a new venture.

Red Tape: High compliance costs associated with unnecessary bureaucratic rules and regulations.

Risk Management: Procedures to identify, quantify and respond to minimise the risks and uncertainties which could prevent the business operating efficiently.

Serendipity: The unexpected discovery of a creative idea or solution to a problem, discovered by accident while looking for something else.

Small Business Management: The management of a small company on a day-to-day basis.

SME: Small Medium (sized) Enterprise - companies with 0-250 employees.

Spin Off Company: When someone leaves an established company to set up a new company to develop new (leading edge) creative ideas.

Stakeholder: Any company or person who has an interest in the venture.

Start up Company: A company formed to implement an opportunity.

Success-Disaster: This occurs when production cannot supply the increasing demand for the product, leading to manufacturing chaos and financial difficulties.

Sustainable Growth: Using retained profits to grow the business.

Venture Capital: Funding provided by investment companies looking for high growth businesses.

Technology Cluster: These develop when a number of companies operating in the same business set up in the same location. This facilitates the cross flow of ideas and sharing of resources.

Triggers and Blocks: Triggers are events and situations that encourage someone to become an entrepreneur, while blocks are situations which prevent someone becoming an entrepreneur.

Book List

Ashton, Robert, *The Entrepreneur's Book of Checklists*, Pearson

Barrow, C., *Incubators*, Wiley

Belbin, Meredith, *Beyond the Team,* Butterworh-Heinemann

Belbin, Meredith, *Management Teams,* Butterworh-Heinemann

Belbin, Meredith, *Team Roles at Work,* Butterworh-Heinemann

Bolton, W. and **Thompson**, B.K., *Entrepreneurs in Focus,* Thomson

Bolton, W.K. and **Thompson**, J.L., *Entrepreneurs - Talent, Temperament, Technique*, Butterworth Heinemann

Branson, Richard, *Losing My Virginity,* Virgin Books

Burke, Rory, *Project Management Planning and Control Techniques (4ed)*, Burke Publishing

Burke, Rory, *Small Business Entrepreneur*, Burke Publishing

Burke, Rory, *Small Project Entrepreneur*, Burke Publishing

Burke, Rory, *Team Building Entrepreneur*, Burke Publishing

Burns, Paul, *Entrepreneurship and Small Business*, Palgrave

Bygrave, W.D., *Portable MBA Entrepreneurship*, Wiley

Carter, Sara, and **Jones-Evans**, Dylan, *Enterprise and Small Business*, FT Prentice Hall

Chaston, Ian, and **Mangles**, Terry, *Small Business Marketing Management*

Chell, E., *Entrepreneurship: Globalisation, Innovation and Development*, Thomson

Christensen, Clayton, *The Innovator's Dilemma, When New Technologies Cause Great Firms to Fail*, Harvard Business School Press

Deakins, D. and **Freel**, Mark, *Entrepreneurship and Small Firms*, McGraw-Hill

De Bono, Edward, *The Use of Lateral Thinking*

Dewhurst, J., **Burns**, P., *Small Business and Entrepreneurship*, MacMillan Press

Drucker, P.F., *Innovation and Entrepreneurship: Practice and Principles*, Heinemann

Fisher, Roger and **Ury**, William, *Getting to Yes: Negotiating Agreement Without Giving In*

Flood, Robert, *Creative Problem Solving*, Wiley

Foley, James, *The Global Entrepreneur*, Dearborn

Frederick, H. & **Kuratko,** D. (2006). *Australasian Entrepreneurship: Theory, Practice and Process,* Thomson Learning

Green, Jim, *Starting Your Own Business,* How To Books

Hall, Craig, *The Responsible Entrepreneur: How to Make Money and Make a Difference,* The Career Press

Harvard Business Essential, *Entrepreneur's Toolkit*, HBS Press

Hisrich, Robert, and **Peter**, Michael, *Entrepreneurship* (5ed), McGraw-Hill

Kirby, David, *Entrepreneurship,* McGraw-Hill

Kuratko, Donald, and **Morris**, Michael, *Corporate Entrepreneurship*, Thomson

Lang, J., *The High-Tech Entrepreneur's Handbook*, FT.com

Legge, John, and **Hindle**, Kevin, *Entrepreneurship Context, Vision and Planning*, Palgrave

Morris, Michael, *The Sunday Times Guide to Starting a Successful Business*, Kogan Page

Morris, M.J., *Successful Expansion for the Small Business*, Kogan Page

Porter, Michael, *The Competitive Advantage of Nations*, MacMillan

Rae, D., *The Entrepreneurial Spirit: Learning to Unlock Value*, Blackhall

Roddick, Anita, *Business As Unusual*, Thorsons

Smith, *Venture Capital*, Independent Publishers Group

Stone, Phil, *Your Own Business: The Complete Guide to Succeeding With a Small Business*, How To Books

Waterworth, D., *Marketing for the Small Business*, MacMillan

Wickham, P.A., *Strategic Entrepreneurship,* Prentice Hall

Williams, Sara, *Lloyds TSB Small Business Guide*, Penguin

Winston, Robert, *The Human Mind*

Index

Fashion Design Series

This *Fashion Design Series* promotes fashion design skills and techniques which can be effectively applied in the world of fashion.

Fashion Computing – Computer Techniques and CAD
Sandra Burke, ISBN: 0-9582391-3-4

This book introduces you to the computer drawing and design skills required by the fashion industry worldwide. Through visuals and easy steps, it explains how to use the most popular graphics software used in the fashion business. It demonstrates fashion drawing, design and presentation techniques and explains how to develop digital communications using powerful computerised tools.

Fashion Artist - Drawing Techniques to Portfolio Presentation
Sandra Burke, ISBN: 0-473-05438-8

Fashion drawing is an essential part of the fashion designer's portfolio of skills. This book is set out as a self-learning programme to teach you how to draw fashion figures and clothing, and present them in a portfolio. The text is supported with explanatory drawings and photographs, together with drawing exercises and worked solutions to speedily aid the learning process.

Fashion Design – Catwalk to Street
Sandra Burke, ISBN: 0-9582391-2-6

This book will help you develop your portfolio of fashion design skills while guiding you through the fashion design process. Starting with the design brief, it explains how to analyse fashion trends, develop a collection, choose fabrics and colorways, create sketchbooks, flats and design presentations. It essentially takes you from concept to creation, and catwalk to street.

Bluewater Trilogy

Be warned - this *Bluewater Trilogy* will inspire you to give it all up to go Bluewater Cruising!

Managing Your Bluewater Cruise
Rory and Sandra Burke, ISBN: 0-473-03822-6, 352 pages

This **preparation guide** discusses a range of pertinent issues from establishing budgets and buying equipment to preventative maintenance and heavy weather sailing. The text works closely with the ORC category 1 requirements and includes many comments from other cruisers who are '*out there doing it*'. So if you wish to bridge the gap between fantasy and reality then your bluewater cruise must be effectively managed.

Greenwich to the Dateline
Rory and Sandra Burke, ISBN: 0-620-16557-x, 352 pages

This is a **travelogue** of our bluewater cruising adventure from the Greenwich Meridian to the International Dateline – sit back with a sundowner and be inspired to cruise to the Caribbean and Pacific islands. In this catalogue of rewarding experiences we describe how we converted our travelling dreams into a bluewater cruising reality.

Bluewater Checklist
Rory and Sandra Burke, ISBN: 0-9582391-0-X, 96 pages

Checklists provide an effective management tool to confirm everything is on board, and all tasks are completed. Why try to remember everything in your head when checklists never forget!!! This book provides a comprehensive portfolio of checklists covering every aspect of bluewater cruising.

Cosmic MBA Series

In our competitive world the successful manager needs Entrepreneurship skills to spot opportunities, and Project Management skills to make-it-happen.

Project Management Planning and Control Techniques (4ed)

Rory Burke
ISBN: 0-9582391-5-0
384 pages

This book presents the latest planning and control techniques, particularly those used by the project management software and the body of knowledge. With sales of 100,000 copies, this book has established itself internationally as the standard text for project management techniques.

Entrepreneurs Toolkit

Rory Burke
ISBN: 0-9582391-4-2
160 pages

Entrepreneurs Toolkit is a comprehensive guide outlining the essential entrepreneur skills to spot a marketable opportunity, the essential business skills to start a new venture and the essential management skills to make-it-happen.

Small Business Entrepreneur

Rory Burke
ISBN: 0-9582391-6-9
160 pages

Small Business Entrepreneur is a comprehensive guide outlining the essential management skills to run a small business on a day-to-day basis.